THINK ON YOUR FEET

Other titles in the *Career Makers* series

DETOX YOUR CAREER
10 steps to revitalizing your job and career
Patrick Forsyth

MANAGE YOUR BOSS
8 steps to creating the ideal working relationship
Patrick Forsyth

NEW KID ON THE BLOCK
10 steps to help you survive and thrive in the first
100 days of your new job
Frances Kay

Forthcoming titles

THERE'S NO NEED TO SHOUT!
10 steps to communicating your message clearly and effectively
Patrick Forsyth

THE GOOD, THE BAD AND THE DOWNRIGHT DIFFICULT
8 steps to dealing with people you'd rather not
Frances Kay

THINK ON YOUR FEET

10 steps to better decision making
and problem solving at work

JEREMY KOURDI

First published in 2006 by:

Marshall Cavendish Business
An imprint of Marshall Cavendish International (Asia) Private Limited
A member of Times Publishing Limited
Times Centre, 1 New Industrial Road
Singapore 536196
T: +65 6213 9300
F: +65 6285 4871
E: te@sg.marshallcavendish.com
Online bookstore: www.marshallcavendish.com/genref

and

Cyan Communications Limited
119 Wardour Street
London W1F 0UW
United Kingdom
T: +44 (0)20 7565 6120
E: sales@cyanbooks.com
www.cyanbooks.com

A CIP record for this book is available from the British Library

ISBN 981 261 825 2 (Asia & ANZ)
ISBN 1-904879-54-3 (Rest of world)

Designed and typeset by Cambridge Publishing Management Limited
Printed and bound in Singapore

To Julie, Tom, and Louise—
great writers, collaborators, and friends.

THE *CAREER MAKERS* SERIES

NEW REALITIES—ESSENTIAL SKILLS

The world of work has never presented people with a greater challenge.

Business pundits and economists predict a range of varying scenarios for the future of the work environment. But one thing all are sure about—the future will be uncertain. We live in dynamic times. The old world of job security, jobs for life, prescribed ladders of promotion, and gradually increasing success and rewards has gone, replaced by talk of reorganization, downsizing (and calling it rightsizing makes it sound no better), redundancy, teleworking, and portfolio careers. Organizations too must recognize new realities and adopt new approaches to stay ahead in an increasingly competitive world.

For the individual, waiting for things to "get back to normal" is simply not one of the options. No one can guarantee a successful career for themselves, though it is something that everyone can influence to some degree. Indeed it is something that you surely *want* to influence. We all spend a great deal of time at work. It is important to make sure that time is as enjoyable and rewarding as possible. There is a line in one of John Lennon's songs: "Life is what happens to you while you're busy making other plans." It encapsulates a painful thought. Situations in which you look back and say something to yourself that begins: "if only . . . " are perhaps the worst possible positions to get into.

With no rigid, pre-ordained career ladder for the individual to follow, the prospects of success cannot be assumed. Similarly, with turbulent markets for organizations to operate in, and dynamic times ahead, no organization can regard success as a given. The bad news is that there is no magic formula guaranteed to ensure overall success. However three things are clear:

- Having the right skills and competencies is the foundation to being able to do your job well

- Surviving and thriving in a competitive workplace demands that you work actively at career development

- Only successful individuals create successful organizations

It is these facts that prompt this series of books. The series takes a positive view, examining a range of areas that are not only valuable to achieving results within a particular job, but are also inherent to making good career progress—it reviews not just business skills, but *career skills*.

So, the individual titles each review their individual topic with an eye on both effectiveness in a job and overall career success. Written by experienced practitioners, they present practical and proven ideas to help you create success in your job, for your organization, and in your career.

Patrick Forsyth

CONTENTS

INTRODUCTION

Decisions and problems can often leave people with a dilemma: knowing that a decision is required, but uncertain how to ensure that it is the best one and that it will be successfully executed. The paradox is that the very pressure for a decision often breeds indecisiveness. In the words of Scott Adams' creation, Dilbert, people all too often feel that: "Indecision is the key to flexibility," and "If at first you don't succeed, destroy all evidence that you tried."

Think on Your Feet addresses this fundamental problem, enabling you to find the best solutions and options, avoid pitfalls, manage risk, work with people to ensure that decisions succeed—and understand how you can improve the way you typically operate when making decisions.

This book provides a practical guide to help you:

- Develop creative, effective options and solutions

- Increase your boldness and confidence when making decisions

- Work with people to implement decisions

- Handle important, complex, or urgent decisions

- Understand how you work best when making decisions and preventing problems

The great thing about decisions is that they are the keys to the future. They provide reassurance, overcoming concerns and challenges. They reduce or remove sources of stress. More positively, they turn problems into opportunities—and they can create opportunities and benefits out of very little.

Perhaps because of their significance, decisions can be demanding or even daunting for many people. We often arrive at decisions quickly, subconsciously, without considering our options—too often we give them too little thought. American President John F. Kennedy recognized this when he said:

> 66 The essence of the ultimate decision remains impenetrable to the observer— often, indeed, to the decider himself . . . There will always be the dark and tangled stretches in the decision-making process—mysterious even to those who may be most intimately involved. 99

This book will help you navigate your way through those dark, tangled stretches, making better decisions and solving problems. Above all, it recognizes that what matters is not how much you know, but how you react to what you do *not* know.

Jeremy Kourdi
2005

step 1

UNDERSTANDING DECISION MAKING AND PROBLEM SOLVING

"The higher we climb, the more comprehensive the view. Each new vantage point yields a better understanding of the interconnection of things. What is more, gradual accumulation of understanding is punctuated by sudden and startling enlargements of the horizon, as when we reach the brow of a hill and see things never conceived of in the ascent. Once we have found our bearings in the new landscape, our path to the most recently attained summit is laid bare and takes its honorable place in the new world."

JULIAN BARBOUR

DECISION MAKING—WHAT IT IS AND WHY IT MATTERS

Decision making is important for many reasons but one of the most important is the fact that it is the route to progress. Whether a decision succeeds or fails, we can learn and benefit. Decision making also highlights the complexity and interconnectedness of things; a vital point to remember and one that makes it so challenging—and interesting.

Problem solving and decision making are central to leadership, work, life, and success. It would not be a stretch to claim that these fundamental human skills define who we are and are what allows us to get things done. Any human endeavor requires someone, first, to overcome a difficulty, make a choice, deal with the consequences, and maintain control over changing circumstances.

For example, America's triumph in the space race is often cited as building upon technical know-how and ingenuity. In fact, it derived from:

- A comparative advantage (relative to the Soviet Union's moon efforts) in making decisions

- An ability to overcome seemingly insurmountable obstacles

- The capacity to deal efficiently with any mistakes made

Most importantly, success in landing the first people on the moon relied on a confidence in eventual victory and an unwillingness to be fazed by the difficulties. This lesson is crucial: most problems persist and most decisions fail to meet aspirations because of a fear of failure, which manifests itself in many different ways.

At a time of increasing interdependence, opportunity, change, competition, and complexity, the importance of making good decisions and solving difficult problems is paramount. And while we hear on a regular basis how important these skills are, we are rarely told what they mean to us on a personal level.

THE PERSONAL NATURE OF DECISION MAKING

People can no longer build personal success around simple solutions and decisions. Considering how much progress mankind has made over the last few centuries, it seems that the only way for an organization or individual to succeed is to have the confidence to leap into the unknown.

The fear of failure must be removed and people must learn to make radical decisions. Mistakenly, decisions are often seen as being either right or wrong, ignoring that what matters is making the best decision from a constellation of choices. All of the available decisions may be right, or may be flawed—the trick is to select the best one.

This book is designed as a guide to making good decisions and solving problems, which will help you in life and in business. More than anything, learning these skills will increase your scarcity—and so your value to society, markets, and employers. Good decision makers and problem solvers are hard to find. By explaining a key aspect of problem solving or decision making, by examining each issue and then including an audit of how you would approach and improve it, you should be able to improve your skills painlessly in these critical areas.

Some of the concepts discussed here are self-evident, whether or not they are practiced, while others are less obvious, and are rarely practiced well or critically. Many of the ideas are novel and a constant theme is the importance of psychology and a corresponding awareness of how we resolve important decisions and problems.

THE PROCESS OF DECISION MAKING

This book treats decisions and problems almost interchangeably, with good reason. Whether an innocuous business decision or a persistent problem—a "wrong" that demands "righting"—it represents an event where one must:

- Generate and appraise multiple options (potential paths that may be taken)

- Evaluate and select the best option

- Implement it in a complex, changing environment subject to the prevailing external forces

The techniques to make this process a success and avoid the inevitable pitfalls are common to all decisions and problems.

BOTH RATIONAL AND INTUITIVE

Another common theme is the importance of being both rational *and* creative and intuitive. The tension and balance between these two styles not only defines our style, but it also colors the outcome of the decision.

INDIVIDUALITY MATTERS

The third theme is the importance of developing an individual style of making decisions and approaching problems. This is preferable to forcing oneself to adopt approaches, styles, and techniques that others value, but which are not appropriate given either the person in question or their unique predicament.

In short, this book will enable you to solve problems, maximize opportunities, and make better decisions.

It is important to understand the different ways decisions are actually made. For example, can you distinguish between a maintenance manager (one who preserves the status quo or reacts to situations) and a visionary leader, capable of anticipating, preventing, or minimizing problems, or turning a problem into an opportunity?

THE BENEFIT OF EXPERIENCE—AND ITS PROBLEMS

Society is built around the principle that experience is the most valuable asset: a good reason why older firms tend to be more respected. However, this only holds up as long as the future resembles the past. The real importance of experience is quite different, and not so often considered. Experience is a valuable asset not because the future closely resembles the past, but because it helps us to understand and cope with change and the unknown.

History teaches us that rather than take lessons from the past into our radically different world, we must learn to cope with uncertainty, with the unknown and be able to act independently. When taking decisions and solving problems, we must be empowered to do so without the comfort of thinking it is easy or that the solution has already been found. People must have the confidence to move beyond "off the shelf" answers and develop their own shelf of solutions.

DECISIONS AND BUSINESS

In a commercial context, decision making means finding new ways to grow revenues and minimize costs so profits are increased, the long-term value of the business is enhanced, and the competitive position of the business is strengthened. These priorities should constantly guide management decisions, influencing the choices that are made throughout the organization.

Decisions are the footfalls of progress: they can be quick or slow, large or small, safe or risky, simple or arduous, but they are the vital components of success.

THE BENEFITS OF ENTREPRENEURIAL DECISIONS

An entrepreneurial decision or solution to a problem is one that creates an opportunity in an original and inventive way. Good entrepreneurial decisions provide organizations with:

● Certainty and decisiveness, preferable to vacillation and drift, as it clarifies what is being done to move toward key goals

● A focus on priority issues, as a proactive approach is being taken

- A competitive advantage by turning a challenging new situation into a unique opportunity to differentiate and excel

- Opportunities—decisions open doors, motivate and energize all the people in the organization

- The means to progress toward strategic objectives

- Greater revenues, fewer costs, increased shareholder value, and long-term prosperity

They also provide the individual with:

- A framework for action, so that effort is not misguided or wasted

- Security and relief from the fear of inaction, indecision, and uncertainty

- An opportunity to display flexibility and ingenuity

SIX STEPS IN DECISION MAKING AND PROBLEM SOLVING

Success in these areas depends on many things, not least the circumstances and available opportunities. However, it is possible to outline a basic framework that may be followed when making decisions and solving problems. This can be perfected and additional considerations and techniques built in to the process to suit your unique requirements, but the framework should help to clarify the general approach to problems and decisions.

Developing a system so that decisions are based on this framework will allow more advanced ideas and tools to be added in later. The framework is built on six sequential steps or best practices:

1. DEFINE THE OBJECTIVE: ASK THE RIGHT QUESTIONS

It is important to ask the right questions. What is the decision trying to achieve? What are the problems? What does it concern? It is often difficult to define a clear objective when there are a number of competing priorities, but there are several possible approaches:

- Decide which objective offers the greatest number of potential benefits or which is the most important. One technique is to ask *why* it is important. What are the benefits?

- Refer to existing policies or plans (for example, a strategic business plan) to see which objective offers the greatest overall benefit

- Seek the views of others and build a consensus about the objective

- Test hypotheses and ideas by asking "If this were the objective, what would be the likely decision and what would be the possible outcome?"

2. COLLECT AND COMPREHEND RELEVANT INFORMATION

Before solutions can be created and plans formulated it is necessary to understand the relevant information and use it. Information failure, as economists say, is the most common cause of failure in all markets. Ask the following questions:

- Do you know *what* information is required to reach a good decision?

- Do you have all the necessary information and expertise to make a quality decision?

- If not, do you know who does have the relevant information, or where it can be found?

- Can you rely on others to help with this decision? Is it reasonable?

- What type of experience is relevant?

Analyzing relevant information can be even harder, and the following techniques are often appropriate:

- Understand and organize the facts, separating them from assumptions or opinions

- Understand the nature of the problem by asking who, what, why, when, where, and how?

- Breaking the whole into its component parts works for complex matters. This means finding the root cause of the problem, working from first principles and identifying the *either/or* upon which many decisions rest

3. DEVELOP PRACTICAL OPTIONS

It is important to be able to choose the best from a number of options, rather than make a decision because there was only one option. Developing multiple options requires a great deal of mental flexibility and imagination. Some ways of going about this are:

- Analyzing the information and reviewing the possible paths to the desired outcome

- Seeking the views of others and brainstorming ideas

- Using creativity and conceptual thinking to imagine possible scenarios and solutions

4. EVALUATE AND SELECT

Evaluate the available options carefully, by considering these key questions:

- What are the risks and potential barriers to success?

- How attractive are the options? (In business this translates to "how profitable are the options?")

- Which decisions are feasible?

- Do the feasible options need to be synthesized into one decision, or could a combination of decisions be taken?

- When is action required?

● What action might be needed to keep options open for the future?

The decision needs to be in line with the objective(s) and overall strategy, should be consistent with other decisions and policies, and must not conflict with other policies or core values. In reaching a decision it can help to work backward from the desired solution to find the decision most likely to bring it about—"reverse engineering" the solution. It can also help to consider whether the problem might solve another problem or issue. Finally, taking a view of the whole area, rather than just the narrow decision that needs to be made, is important in maintaining an overall sense of perspective.

5. IMPLEMENT

It is essential that the practical implementation of the decision is appreciated: where, how, and when the objective will be realized. Ask who will make it happen, who is responsible, and what is their incentive? There is little point in reaching decisions if they are unworkable or misunderstood, as this can lead to decisions being poorly implemented and failing. Communication is critical, as successful implementation will require everyone to understand their role and carry it out well.

6. MONITOR AND MODIFY

Making a decision and then sticking with it is often important, but this needs to be tempered with an ability to recognize when the situation has moved on and a new decision is required. No decision or solution to a problem is perfect and as it plays out in the real world there is no shame in using new experience to improve it. Final success is what matters, rather than initial success. Monitoring the effects of the decision will provide useful information for its continued implementation and success, as well as for future decisions. Developing systems so that the practical implementation of the decision can be modified at different times is fundamental to modern, heuristic ways of decision making.

HANDLING DECISION-MAKING CHALLENGES

There are several fundamental difficulties with decision making:

- Decisions are rarely straightforward or simple. This is because they frequently rely upon intangible forces, such as people's attitudes and perceptions, and they may rest upon assumptions

- Decisions invariably involve value judgments, risks, and uncertainties

- There are difficulties involved in evaluating the long-term consequences of decisions

The need to solve problems quickly and effectively arises throughout organizations and it is closely related to decision making. Both involve a logical and systematic approach to defining the problem, generating possible solutions, choosing, and then implementing the best option. However, there are difficulties and hidden traps within problem solving, such as the danger of over-analysis. Often, what is really required is nothing more than a pen, paper, and a period of quiet thought and discussion.

Decisions that involve customers and markets are among the most complicated and demanding of all. Markets, customers, and competitors all constantly develop and change, yet the vital importance of marketing decisions for the health and prosperity of the organization remains unaltered.

UNDERSTANDING SIGNIFICANT DECISIONS

Often, what matters with significant decisions is not only what is actually decided, but also *how* the decision is reached and implemented. Military decisions provide a case in point: clearly any decision to go to war needs careful, sensitive analysis. All options should be considered and there is necessarily a detailed process leading up to the final, transparent decision. And this is not the end: the most critical phase of a decision is its implementation. It is essential to pay constant attention to detail throughout the process, always keeping in mind the final objective. With some decisions, mistakes can be rectified later; with critical decisions, mistakes are usually much, much harder to recover from.

> To paraphrase Winston Churchill, once the decision has been made it is neither the end nor the beginning of the end, but it is the end of the beginning.

One of the keys to making critical decisions effectively is to trust your judgment and accept responsibility. There is a tendency to look for scapegoats or to shift responsibility (or even blame, should things go wrong), or else to avoid making the decision. Even if these negative attitudes subsequently change they can seriously undermine both the decision and its implementation, for example, by alienating people and reducing credibility. Confidence is important because it leads to commitment and a clear, focused approach, and confidence implies trusting one's judgment and accepting responsibility. Once in the right frame of mind and having collated the right tools to make a successful decision based upon both intuitive and rational "best practices," successful decision makers must master four important activities:

1. COMMITTING

While it is always worth being a realist and considering contingency measures, fail-safe decisions, and fallback positions, it is also important to remain committed and loyal to the decision. Critical decisions are often subject to close, in-depth analysis, criticism, and even ridicule or abuse, perhaps because they are so important and emotive; in these circumstances any wavering or lack of commitment can quickly cause the decision and its implementation to unravel.

2. COMPREHENDING

Thoroughness is frequently sacrificed at the expense of time and this is an obvious danger with critical decisions. There is a danger of *paralysis by analysis* (of which more later), but the opposite is also hazardous: the belief that research is unnecessary or irrelevant. For example, the common denominators of a successful business are its people, products, markets, profit, and cash flow. While there is a tendency to focus on decisions affecting the first three, people often fear and neglect financial skills and decisions. It is important to complete each stage of the decision-making process thoroughly, and for major commercial decisions this may well involve using financial techniques such as forecasting or ratio analysis.

3. RISKING

Actively managing and minimizing the risk in decision making is essential at all times—but never more so than with critical decisions. In the run-up to the decision, consider how the level of risk can be reduced, not only in terms of increasing the likelihood of success but also by considering what can be done if things start going adrift. This might involve getting the support of others or at least taking time to explain how you have reached your decision. Having minimized the risk, it is important to understand that no success can be made without risk. Building a personal ability to accept risk without it affecting either your performance or the performance of other areas of operations is essential to getting good returns.

4. SEEING BEYOND THE "TUNNEL"

Taking a wider view and avoiding tunnel vision in selecting any specific option is an important step in achieving success with critical decisions. Considering the wider impact of a decision will help to make sure that the right choice is being made and that it is being implemented most effectively. Unfortunately, this process of reviewing external factors is often seen mistakenly as a sign of weakness. In truth, avoiding tunnel vision demands:

- Considering the effects of the decision on others

- Understanding the factors that will influence how the decision will work in practice

- Acknowledging people's expectations and the culture of the environment in which the decision is being made

- Having an appreciation of past events and any relevant background details

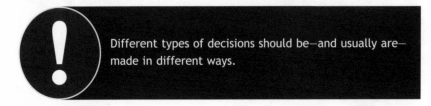

Different types of decisions should be—and usually are—made in different ways.

INTRODUCING DECISION-MAKING PITFALLS

Knowing where and when decisions usually fail is essential to ensuring your decisions don't "run aground" in the same areas. It is even more important to know the most common reasons why decisions may fail. These include:

PARALYSIS BY ANALYSIS

This means too much analysis and discussion when what is required is action. The paralysis can be caused by over-monitoring the situation, not seeing its boundaries, or constantly focusing on defensive measures. For example, if you are drowning it does not help to measure the depth of the water, to know whether other people are also drowning, or even to understand how you came to be in the water in the first place. All of these are excellent questions. But if you are drowning, the single priority has to be survival: and all actions and decisions need to reflect this.

Consequently, organizations must focus on eliminating what Sir John Harvey Jones, among others, terms *paralysis by analysis*—the tendency to analyze competing options without ever actually reaching a decision. Whether this tendency occurs when there is a high-risk factor, such as during critical decisions, or is a trait in the personality of the individual making the decision, it results in decisions drifting. It is perfectly acceptable—even advisable—to take one's time and analyze, consider, and discuss, but there comes a time to act and this point in the process needs to be recognized.

There may be good reasons to be risk averse, but fear of failure should not be one of them. Leaders need to be aware of the consequences of delay, and they also need to possess the courage to decide.

THE KNOWING–DOING GAP

This concept, coined by Jeffrey Pfeffer and Robert Sutton, is similar to paralysis by analysis, except the emphasis is less on finding out what has happened and more on finding solutions, discussing options, planning the best approach . . . but not ever actually *realizing* those solutions. What should be done is known; it is just never actually done!

A variety of this is when action is taken, but is insufficient to meet the needs of the situation. For example, in the 1980s senior executives at Xerox decided that the priorities were to reduce costs and raise customer satisfaction. According to information from Harvard Business School, a comprehensive quality initiative lasting four years was launched in which employees at almost every level discussed the quality initiative. 70,000 employees received approximately six days of training each, yet at the end of the process few concrete decisions had been made affecting the company's products, and attitudes to quality had not improved much either. For example, Harvard reported that only 15% of employees said they believed that recognition and rewards were based on quality improvements, and only 13% reported using cost-of-quality analyses in their decision making.

IGNORANCE, ERRORS, AND MISTAKES

With paralysis by analysis and the knowing-doing gap, the best that can be said is that people are at least aware that things are not right, and are working—albeit inadequately—to improve them. This carries with it the chance of success: the possibility of change to deliver improvements.

More often, however, organizations do not even get that far. Although the necessary information is available, the staff are either complacent or simply fail to see the problem signs. This may arise from a culture of blame, low responsibility, poor communication, inadequate systems for managing information and knowledge, departure of key staff, human error, distraction, or any of a number of factors. Whatever the cause, the result is clear: ignorance of the real issues and the need for effective decisions.

Organizations, therefore, need to ensure that they have the necessary systems in place to capture accurate information about both internal and external factors, for people to understand what to do. This means regularly reviewing and analyzing that information and agreeing what action is needed to keep in pursuit of the organization's objectives.

INFORMATION OVERLOAD

Information is being created and supplied at a rapidly expanding rate, driven largely by technological developments such as the growth of computing power and the Internet. The danger is not that there is too little information, but rather that there is too much superfluous data obscuring the relevant and important details. This in turn makes it harder to accomplish the tasks of analysis and decision making. The solution is to implement a process for effective information management that incorporates analyzing data in core areas, storing the relevant information, supplying information to the right person at the right time, and, of course, acting on the information.

The next chapter will enable you to develop your personal style when approaching critical decisions and will clarify the different ways that people make decisions.

step ②

ASSESSING YOUR
DECISION-MAKING STYLE

"The reasonable man adapts himself to the world: the unreasonable one persists in trying to adapt the world to himself. Therefore all progress depends on the unreasonable man."

GEORGE BERNARD SHAW

HOW WE MAKE DECISIONS

The significance of the decisions made by decision makers and problem solvers is inversely proportional to the number that they make. Senior executives tend to make only a few, albeit important, decisions, while those on the front line frequently need to make decisions. While the senior executives' decisions grab the headlines and attention, less senior people can often have a more important effect by changing perceptions as well as determining the success or failure of the operation.

How people make decisions does not simply depend on rank: it depends on the individual's experiences.

There are many broad styles of making a decision—one way of differentiating between people's styles is between those that decide rationally and those that decide intuitively. Management theorist Peter Drucker believes decision making to be a *rational* process. That is, it relies on a set of sequential steps leading to the desired outcome. A framework is set for reaching an effective decision, with failure coming as a consequence of deviation from this framework or of the inadequacies of the framework itself.

RATIONAL . . .

A typical rational approach is to:

1. **Assess the situation.** Rational decision makers ask whether the decision relates to an underlying issue, or whether it is the result of an isolated event. Generic decisions need to be addressed consistently, while isolated events are exceptional. If the problem is one that has recurred, or will do so, then an "off the shelf" solution will suffice. If the problem is unique, then unique thinking is demanded.

2. **Define and specify the decision.** This ensures the problem is understood first. The best way to go about this is to clarify the parameters for success.

3. **Make the decision.** Effective decision makers understand the need to compromise to achieve the essential goals. Nevertheless, the decision maker needs to have a clear view of what is right and do what is needed, without hesitation or failure. It is this stage that can benefit greatly from creativity and innovation.

4. **Implement the decision.** This is the key stage: making it happen. Executing the decision is the most time-consuming, critical phase, demanding flexibility and unflagging attention.

5. **Monitor the decision, making adjustments.** There are two certainties: decisions concern fallible people, and they are made in a changing environment. Reporting procedures should be built into the process to monitor the implementation of the decision. As circumstances change, and mistakes are made, solutions can be perfected.

However, it is important to understand that just as intuition and emotion may result in irrationality, so too can issues at the other end of the spectrum. An emphasis on rationality can lead to an ignorance of creative insight and a lack of emotional intelligence. Inept problem solvers are terrorized by problems, using the very process of solving them to hide from them and create "noise" to distract from the real task at hand. The key is balance. In the words of Michael Eisner, for many years the CEO of the Walt Disney Company: "Balanced emotions are crucial to intuitive decision making."

When making decisions or solving problems, emotions must be understood and managed actively because, like it or not, they are important.

. . . OR INTUITIVE?

Events are not always ordered or clear, and relevant information may be unavailable. This can prohibit rational decisions. People may not think consistently and may make mistakes. Anyway, aren't insight, random moments of genius, and creativity valuable? And what is the point of a rational process when reality undermines it? A rational approach only provides the framework; what's required are inspiration, insight, and instinct. The intuitive approach is the use of individual perspectives to dictate decisions. It is best to view rationality as the "macro" framework and intuition as providing the "micro" detail and ingenuity.

Many decisions are ambiguous—concerned with choices, not absolute rights or wrongs. Quantitative methods are usually used earlier in people's careers, but lose their relevance as decisions become more complex and a matter of personality. All successful people, at some point, go beyond the numbers. Sound instinct is what employers are paying for.

WHEN MAKING DECISIONS . . .

- Balancing emotions *and* reason is necessary to make successful decisions

- The rational approach provides a check on the application of instinct, which can run away with itself in a welter of fear, lack of confidence, or excitement

- Instinct balances the sterile uniformity of the rational approach. Together with intuition and emotion, it can be used to bring flair and insight, which lead to the best decision

THE ROLES WE PLAY

Experience suggests that decision makers are placed in as many different situations as there are people to make decisions! However, we can generalize, grouping people into several distinct types of decision maker.

There is no "right" or "wrong" way to make a decision, as each decision demands different approaches for it to turn into a success. To be more scientific, we can say that people exhibit clear behavioral preferences when making decisions. These must be understood as different approaches suit different circumstances.

The following represent some of the personalities that people adopt when decision making and some of the approaches people prefer to take. Do you recognize these people around you—at work and in life generally? Considering the strengths and weaknesses of each approach should enable you to synthesize a wiser and more effective style of decision making and problem solving.

THE POLITICIAN

This approach emphasizes debate, discussion, and consensus. The Politician is likely to go with the majority and emphasize the people aspects of making and implementing decisions.

Strengths:

- Seeks a wide range of opinions and ideas from people

- Attempts to build a consensus about the best approach

- Works well in group situations (like politics!)

Weaknesses:

- Can upset and alienate people if consensus is not possible and one approach has to be chosen above another

- The quality of the decision can depend on the quality of the ideas available

THE ROBOT

This person rigidly follows policies and procedures: they clearly understand what is expected of them and know that there is little or no room for deviation. This approach works well for people in extremely stressful or high-pressured situations: soldiers, surgeons, or certain aspects of the emergency services.

Strengths:

- Clear and focused

- Risk averse

- Accurate and thorough

- No need for explanation or discussion

Weaknesses:

- Little or no scope for creativity or initiative

- If the procedures or frameworks are flawed, then so are the resulting decisions and actions

THE COWBOY

Shooting from the hip is the style adopted by this decision maker. They often make quick, "snap" decisions and then actively focus on implementing them and making them work. They are loyal to decisions once made, and can be tough and uncompromising.

Strengths:

- Prepared to take difficult decisions

- Willing to see their decisions through to their conclusion

- Clear and focused

- Leads from the front

- Consistent—unlikely to change course once a decision has been made. Getting the result is all that matters: invariably the ends are seen as justifying the means

Weaknesses:

- Can be insensitive and inappropriate: not a team approach

- Generates an emotive response from others: respect or dislike, liking or loathing

THE LONG-DISTANCE RUNNER

This decision-making style is relentless and uncompromising: the need to attain the objective is paramount and is pursued with a never-say-die attitude. They cannot be stopped and they simply will not give up—ever.

Strengths:

- Relentless and determined

- Resourceful, competitive, and completely unwilling to accept failure

- Innovative and particularly strong at generating options and solutions

- Works well when their back is against the wall—this approach often encourages and inspires others to new achievements

Weaknesses:

- Works well in difficult or changing situations, but is less suited to normal or mundane conditions

- Can be ruthless in their pursuit of the ultimate objective

THE HISTORIAN

This approach looks to past events and precedents for the right decision. Best practice is understood and brought to bear when decisions are required: this might be in the process of analysis, decision making itself, or implementing the decision.

Strengths:

- Able to see potential flaws early and take preemptive action

- Values experience and works well in similar or repetitive situations (for example, a lawyer or accountant)

- Emphasizes information and data—primary sources—and avoids conjecture or snap decisions

Weaknesses:

- Less well-suited to new situations, although the historian may recognize the need for innovation when it arises

- Decisions may lack initiative, or be wrong if affected by a mistaken interpretation of events

THE MAVERICK

This style is quirky and unusual: people who adopt this approach often have an idiosyncratic way of viewing situations and might be good lateral thinkers. They also tend to dislike rules and approach things in their own individual way.

Strengths:

- Ingenious and intelligent

- Questions established norms and rules—likes to "think outside the box" (similar to the Long-distance Runner in this respect)

- Hugely innovative

- Questions authority

Weaknesses:

- Decisions are the key—effective implementation is often a secondary concern

- Decisions may be fine in theory but hard to make work in practice

MIXING STYLES

For people to meet all of their challenges successfully, the ideal approach is to adopt a complex and varied *mix of styles*. Clearly, an appreciation of these various styles is extremely valuable, but individual decision makers need to consider the specific demands of their current position, and then clarify, establish, sustain, and change their approach as required.

This is fundamental to decision making, especially in organizations. If leaders are unable or unwilling to change their style and the organization's competencies to cope with the dynamic, turbulent, competitive environment, then the organization—or possibly just the individual—will fail.

> While continuous improvement is always valued in organizations, there are also times when a more dramatic, discontinuous change is needed.

Decision makers increasingly understand that, in addition to strategic leadership skills and the ability to manage uncertainty, they must also possess *an ability to manage in adversity*, whether resulting from the loss of an existing market, a crisis of confidence among customers, the failure of a business product, or some other factor. The organization's structure, culture, and control systems need to be flexible enough to allow for emergency decision making and swift, remedial action to overcome these difficulties.

ADOPTING THE BEST STYLE WHEN MAKING DECISIONS

- The enlightened decision maker or successful problem solver will adopt different styles at different times. They have the perceptiveness to realize when a particular style will work, why, and in sufficient time to permit action to be taken

- People often combine aspects of a particular approach—the key is to know what elements of each approach to use, and when

- People's decision-making approaches tend to focus on a single style, which categorizes that person and is largely the result of human nature. This is not necessarily "bad"—after all, a person's value derives from their unique approach. However, decision making can be improved by learning to adopt methods that represent a break from one's "norm"

- Using the right decision-making style requires sensitivity to the situation. Be aware that the nuances of each situation are often unfamiliar or unexpected

- There is a need for effective leadership during the process of decision making. This applies throughout the organization, and includes those managers responsible for specific functions as well as the overall leader

- Decision makers must learn to manage uncertainty: this requires an ability not only to be proactive, but also to respond effectively to events. As we said at the start, it is not simply what we know that matters, but how we react to what we do not know

- Decision making in organizations requires a broad awareness and understanding of what is happening. The commercial environment is becoming increasingly volatile, competitive, and international, driven by many factors including the widespread application of technology. The potential for chaos exists and organizations must find ways of dealing with constant challenges

AUDITING YOUR DECISION-MAKING STYLE

By answering the following questions, you will:

- Clarify the styles you prefer to adopt when making decisions

- Understand the strengths and weaknesses of the different approaches

The questions in the table on page 42 are designed to assess skills in specific aspects of decision making. While some questions can be answered "wrongly" and so would require some remedial action to be taken, most questions are not simply "black and white." Consequently, they allow you to understand your strengths and weaknesses, and represent areas you might wish to improve.

Rate each question on a scale from 1 to 5, where: 1 is never, 2 is seldom, 3 is sometimes, 4 is often, 5 is always.

Your style	1	2	3	4	5
1. Do you define your objectives before making major decisions?					
2. Do you apply a range of approaches to decision making?					
3. Do you use technology to improve the decision making process (e.g. to research facts or test solutions)?					
4. When making decisions with others do you agree the objective first?					
5. How often do you check that you have all the necessary information?					
6. Do you take time to analyze information before making decisions?					
7. Do you generate multiple solutions during the decision-making process?					
8. Do you evaluate each of the various options, and their associated risks?					
9. Do you meticulously prepare the implementation of major decisions?					
10. Do you monitor decisions after they have been made?					
11. Do you support decisions with further actions and decisions?					
12. Are you confident in your ability to make major decisions?					
Total:					

A score of 50 or more indicates a clear, consistent, and methodical approach to decision making.

Scores between 40 and 50 show a clear tendency to approach major decisions in a thorough and conscientious manner, aware of the need to focus on most elements of the decision-making process. However, there may be areas for improvement, with certain parts of the process sometimes being neglected.

Scores between 30 and 40 suggest that the approach is sound, but there are areas where definite improvements can be made. Review your decision-making approach to see where attention is needed.

Scores between 25 and 30 demand greater consistency. Perhaps decisions are being approached intuitively. If so, this may work well, but there is a need to focus on the neglected stages of the decision-making process.

Scores of less than 25 can show a haphazard approach: decisions may work out, but there is no assurance of consistency. Even if decisions are being made and implemented, their quality could be improved with adherence to the decision-making process.

The next chapter will:

- Outline a framework for successful problem solving

- Increase the speed and quality of your problem solving

- Enable you to use the right problem-solving technique at the right time

- Help you understand the strengths and weaknesses of different techniques

- Give you confidence in your ability to solve problems successfully

step 3

PROBLEM-SOLVING
TECHNIQUES

"An expert problem solver must be endowed with two incompatible qualities—a restless imagination and a patient pertinacity."

HOWARD W. EVES

A PROBLEMATIC WORLD

Stepping away, for a moment, from analyzing decisions, it is worth considering how you approach problems and how you respond to the difficulties you face.

First, consider the range of problems you face. Problems can be positive or negative: problems that are to do with opportunities and building success, or those that are concerned with minimizing failure, or "damage control." Second, find the most appropriate way to distinguish between problems—and find the right solution.

The need to solve problems quickly and effectively is closely related to decision making. Both involve a logical and systematic approach to:

- Defining the problem

- Generating possible solutions

- Choosing and then implementing the best option

THE DANGERS OF OVER-ANALYSIS

There is a danger when problem solving of *over-analysis*. Sometimes, all that is required is a pen, paper, and a period of quiet thought and discussion. If the problem is difficult, or just important, it might be prudent to add a team of trusted people to this list.

Just as there are leadership styles so there are problem-solving styles: methods or processes that successful leaders regularly rely on to resolve difficult issues.

THE IMPORTANCE OF PEOPLE

Common to both problem solving and decision making is the need to get the best from people; unlocking people's creative abilities is of vital importance. Everyone has the capacity to be creative.

47

Remember that, outside work, individuals are hugely creative, for example, bringing up children, pursuing hobbies, and generally contributing to society; why not harness those skills at work? People want to realize their creative potential. Also, organizations require creativity and innovation for success, as much to keep pace with the rapid rate of change as to solve problems.

THE NEED FOR PRACTICALITY

The practical element of this is important. While many manuals extol the importance of decision making, they often ignore two things:

1. There is a need for strategies to deal with smaller, more common problems as well as the larger ones that define an organization's core values and long-term strategies.

2. There is a conspicuous lack of practical advice given to people on how to deal with problems.

Problem solving is about responding within the real world; understanding and analyzing problems and their causes is only a relatively small part of any solution.

THE PROBLEM-SOLVING PROCESS

There are a number of steps to follow (or to encourage others to follow) when problem solving:

1. **Overcome barriers.** This means not being afraid to recognize that problems exist, and being prepared to take action quickly before the difficulty spreads or deepens. The leader therefore needs to create a blame-free environment where problems are openly acknowledged. More than this, there needs to be an environment that values planning and actively prevents and pre-empts difficulties.

2. **Define the problem.** The scope and scale of the problem needs to be clearly understood. This can be done by asking the key questions of what, when, where, how, and who? It is worth remembering that unwelcome events may occur, but unless they cause ongoing difficulties or something can be done about them, then they may not necessarily be *problems*.

3. **Gather relevant information.** Find out details so that the causes and possible solutions emerge and can be acted on.

4. **Identify causes.** This will help to highlight where the action needs to be taken as well as what that action needs to be.

5. **Identify possible solutions.** This involves getting to the root of the problem rather than merely tackling the symptoms, and using whatever techniques are best to generate solutions.

6. **Make the decision.** This is perhaps the simplest part of the process: select the most promising option, plan its implementation, and then stick with it.

7. **Monitor the results.** There is often a time lag between the moment decisions are made or implemented, and the moment that they start to take effect. If this is the case, then the best approach is to keep faith in the original choice. However, you need to be able to recognize early if things are not going as planned—either because of poor planning or implementation— and take corrective action. Even with the best choices, further decisions and adjustments may be needed to keep things on course.

USING GROUPS TO SOLVE PROBLEMS

BENEFITS OF GROUPS FOR SOLVING PROBLEMS

Groups are both a technique for solving problems and a source of additional problems! Using a team of people to solve a problem, usually through discussion and then consensus, gives certain benefits including:

- Experience and expertise is shared so that additional insight is gained

- The diverse experience of others allows people to learn from each other, creating a unique learning experience and enhancing the quality of future decisions

- Most people have access to only a finite number of resources, so that more people will mean more resources. Ask yourself how you define a resource—do you count only physical ones (such as capital or information systems) or softer ones too (such as contacts and networks or even life experience)?

- New ideas can be generated when people brainstorm by building on each others' ideas until the best option is reached

- Ideas can be tested and discussed

- Groups can provide mutual support and encouragement to build confidence; this is critical if a decision needs patience for success

- Responsibility and workload is shared, minimizing individual risk and stress

HARNESSING THE BENEFITS OF GROUPS FOR DECISION MAKING

Research suggests that in some situations, the crowd collectively is smarter than any of its individuals for making decisions—even the smartest. While there will always be someone smarter than the crowd in any given run, those individuals will vary from run to run, unable to repeat their success consistently.

In order to harness this collective knowledge, three conditions must obtain:

- There must be a means of aggregating the results

- Individual decisions must be made independently

- The decisions must be unbiased, uninfluenced by an outside bias pushing the crowd in one direction

The first condition makes the results useful, the second keeps the crowd from turning into a mob, and the third prevents a dictator from manipulating that mob.

In his book, *The Wisdom of Crowds*, James Surowiecki identifies three different kinds of problem: cognition, coordination, and cooperation.

- Crowds are best at solving cognitive problems on their own

- Coordination problems require a feedback mechanism

- Cooperation problems, by far the most interesting, can require an entire social structure to enforce certain norms and incentives

PROBLEMS WITH GROUP PROBLEM SOLVING

In spite of the above benefits, many people ignore the downsides of working with people and, consequentially, seek external help, guidance, support, and insight on too regular a basis. This is to ignore both the high demands of working with others, as opposed to working solo, and the pitfalls of groups—though, if properly understood, these can be overcome.

The pitfalls of group problem solving include:

- **Groupthink** (see also p. 169) occurs when a herd mentality prevails, so that people follow one approach unquestioningly, giving credence and additional impetus to the *wrong* decision. The herd mentality actually reduces the time given to questioning and rational consideration of options and can occur if there is a fear of criticism in the group

- **Individuals can be demotivated** if their views are ignored, even coming to obstruct the problem-solving process

- **Implementing the decision can become difficult** if members of the group become informed opponents of the decision, or if they switch loyalties (for example, to a competitor). This can spawn more problems than there were in the first place!

- **Groups can become competitive**—perhaps between different factions or leaders—and while this may be helpful at times, it is much more likely to cause problems if sustained for any length of time. This may happen if core people in the group are in some form of contest with each other—say, for promotion

- **There can be a lack of an overall leader driving the process.** Many tasks can be shared, but invariably there will need to be a leader. People in groups subconsciously recognize their need for leadership, and one of the fascinating features of any group is to see the emergence of a leader. This is inevitable, but rarely acknowledged at the start of process—leaving a chaotic contest for primacy that actually solves nothing

TEN TECHNIQUES FOR GROUP-BASED PROBLEM SOLVING

To avoid these pitfalls and for successful group-based problem solving, it is valuable to understand ten important techniques:

1. **Agreeing the aims of the group.** It is clearly vital for everyone to be pulling in the same direction and this direction needs to be clearly agreed from the outset.

2. **Allowing leaders to emerge.** Remember that leaders will always emerge from a group of individuals. The time needed for this to happen—and the effectiveness of their decisions—will relate directly to the maturity of the group. A well-established team will obviously work more efficiently than a newly assembled group that are still struggling to understand each other.

3. **Using the right information for the job.** It is vital to know exactly what information is needed to make a particular decision, who has it, and where it is to be found. Confusion will cause fractures to emerge within the group. There is a role for delegation here but the important point is to be comprehensive and have all the relevant facts. If information is missing then this must be appreciated: to ignore it is to risk seriously undermining any strategy that is developed.

4. **Using the decision to develop team skills.** Clearly, this works best in relatively low-risk situations, or where the team has attained a high degree of expertise, experience, and autonomy. Once these skills have evolved, future sessions of group problem solving will be far easier.

5. **Assessing how important the problem is.** If vital, then the leader may well want to take it on completely themselves. Tasks and authority may be delegated but ultimate responsibility rests clearly with the leader. It is unfair to ask team members to carry responsibilities that are not theirs—and anyway, teams often have a habit of dumping poor leaders! If, as a leader, you feel happy for the team to decide on the solution and are willing to accept any consequences that may follow, then this is definitely the approach to take.

6. **Building a team with the necessary levels of expertise and commitment for success.** If the team members have the appropriate skills, then the best approach may well be to support and encourage them in making the decision; if they do not, then a better approach would be to develop the skills of the team in general and individuals in particular before considering the decision.

7. **Using personal commitment to generate commitment from others.** Many factors determine the degree to which groups should participate in problem solving. Chief among these are the maturity of the group, the nature of the problem, and the background to the situation. Allowing people to take part can ensure that they are mobilized and committed to the task in hand.

8. **Using group momentum.** This is better than trying to artificially facilitate a productive environment. Problem solving benefits from a dynamic, active approach, and generating a sense of momentum in a group is a useful means of overcoming potential obstacles. Momentum also helps to mobilize people and it is a subtle way of exerting pressure so that people

perform to their best. The alternative is to stagnate, perhaps leading to paralysis by analysis. One of the advantages of groups is their ability to generate impetus and momentum.

9. **Getting the best from people.** Group dynamics are notoriously complicated but it is wise to use the resources of every individual. Talents and expertise lie dormant within each person. These can be uncovered by creating the right environment for the group, providing support, encouraging mutual support and participation, challenging individuals in a positive way, fostering confidence, and building on successes.

10. **Reaching a consensus.** Consensus is vital. The alternative is non-participation, tacit disapproval, or outright disagreement and these are clearly divisive, frustrating, and certain to prevent success. These are problems demanding complicated solutions in their own right! The group should agree how the goal will be achieved and the solution implemented once a strategy has been formulated.

DELEGATING PROBLEM SOLVING

Effective delegation is essential for problem solving, as, once you have developed a strategy, you will need a number of people to implement it. Thus the success or failure of the decision invariably rests with the delegation process. Empowerment goes beyond simply delegating a specific task: it is about granting a defined level of authority and area of responsibility within which someone solves their own problems and then implements their decisions.

Effective delegation is about being competent at each of the following stages:

● **Preparing to delegate.** This involves focusing on results and having clear, precise objectives. It may also involve preparation and planning, gaining the approval of others, or simply informing people. You may also need to consider which are your priorities

- **Matching person and task.** Clearly, the person who is required to do the job must understand it and have the personal skills and competency to have a realistic chance of success, even if it is different, important, or challenging

- **Discussing and agreeing objectives.** The task needs to be carefully talked through from purpose through to fulfillment, so that targets, resources, review times, and deadlines are agreed. It may also be necessary to check understanding and gain explicit agreement to the decision and the planned approach

- **Providing resources and the appropriate level of authority.** When delegating, it is absolutely essential to provide all the necessary resources as well as the authority to complete the task, and then to provide support and backup when needed. To do otherwise is to risk failure and undermine the likelihood that the decision will be properly implemented. Clearly defining responsibilities is also important

- **Monitoring progress.** The key to monitoring is to ensure that the person completing the task remains accountable. Delegation without either accountability or control is simply abdication. This certainly does not mean interfering, distracting, or undermining, but it often means checking progress at pre-planned and specified times to verify that things are on track

- **Reviewing and assessing overall progress.** A final review provides a chance for both the manager and subordinate to learn for the future. This is best done by reviewing achievements against the original, overall objectives

We have ignored the most important technique for problem solving and the one with probably the most consequences for improving the problem-solving process: developing creativity and innovation. For many people the notion of generating ideas and solutions that can form the basis for successful decisions is daunting and extremely difficult. The answer often lies in *fostering* innovation—creating the right conditions and providing prompts and stimuli so that other people can share the creative burden. (Innovation will be discussed further in Step 8.)

UNDERSTANDING PROBLEMS

It is useful to understand how problems usually emerge and to be able to distinguish between different types of problem. The two main types of problem are:

1. **Programmed problems.** These are usually the problems that occur as a routine part of a manager's job. Even when they are complex and require careful deliberation, the solutions are often found by following organizational precedent and procedures. Examples include machine breakdown, salary and staff dilemmas, and budget issues. Linear programming, queuing theory, and decision-tree techniques are methods that can be used to deal with programmed problems.

2. **Non-programmed problems.** These are problems that are central to strategy and for which no single system or procedure determines the right course of action. They may involve anything from development of new products to the shape of a marketing campaign—and they are usually of fundamental importance to the success of particular product lines, or even an organization itself. The most common, but not always the most effective, technique for solving non-programmed problems is creative problem solving, including brainstorming (see p. 134).

CAUSE AND EFFECT ANALYSIS

This technique uses an understanding of the problem to extrapolate a solution logically. Essentially, this involves determining the effects of the problem in order to work out what the actual problem is and to find a solution. For example, when treating a patient, a doctor observes the symptoms to decide what the problem is.

Cause and effect analysis proceeds with the following steps:

- **Label the problem.** This means expressing its effects in sufficient detail that others can also identify what it is. Labels connect effects to possible causes. If the effect is a 10% increase in late deliveries of goods, then connect this to possible causes of this problem, for example, problems with people, poor transport, inefficient order systems, and limited product availability

- **Identify the root causes of the problem.** The most common are to do with people, materials, and equipment. Others may include circumstances or historical factors. For example, if late product delivery is because of poor communication, then communications systems or excessive bureaucracy are potential problems

- **Collect data on the causes of the problem.** Asking the staff involved their opinions should help pin down the cause or causes, which can then be dealt with

CHOOSING YOUR SOLUTION

Solutions are often mistakenly seen as being either right or wrong, ignoring the fact that what matters most is making the best decision from a set of choices. In certain instances all of the available decisions may be right, or they may all be flawed; the important point is to select the best available option.

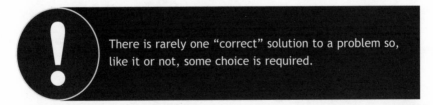

There is rarely one "correct" solution to a problem so, like it or not, some choice is required.

Analysis is one of the least popular areas of problem solving. People naturally gravitate toward a particular option because of a complex array of factors that are often totally irrational and quite possibly destructive to the situation. These may include prejudice, fear (especially fear of change), desire to avoid risk, laziness, or an over-reliance on instinct.

The are two main techniques for dealing with a situation where a solution is required but where there is also some degree of choice, or where the correct answer may be ambiguous.

LISTING AND ASSESSING YOUR GOALS AND OBJECTIVES

First, list the most important goals, then rule out those strategies that cannot accomplish your goals or favor those that meet all the relevant criteria and that are the easiest to implement. This is inherently a rational process and is probably most appropriate if the problem solver[s] have relatively better skills of analysis than practical experience: in other words, where a more intuitive process would fail.

This technique works by first selecting criteria for the final decision through a brainstorming process (it needs to work quickly, not be expensive or take much time to organize), and then proceeding to score each option against these criteria on a scale from 1 to 10. The highest scoring option wins. Problem solving can often be done best by removing emotional commitment to certain strategies and, instead, playing it as a game. Conversely, at other times, the emotional commitment can be an asset, driving us to previously unthinkable solutions. What works best is entirely a function of the situation.

PRIORITIZING YOUR CHOSEN GOALS AND OBJECTIVES

The second technique is probably the more common, irrespective of whether it is right for the situation, because of the psychology of most problem solvers. This is where one settles on the most important goal for the strategy, and picks the solution that most efficiently and sustainably serves this single goal. This simple approach is almost always complicated by the need to weigh goals up against each other, reduce costs, and minimize risk. This method can lack the thorough assessment of a variety of options that the first technique deploys.

Once your goals are clearly understood and have been prioritized, the next challenge is to find ways to generate solutions to your problem.

IMPLEMENTING THE SOLUTION

Once you have come up with a list of possible solutions and selected one for implementation, the focus shifts to successfully executing the decision. This is usually the most time-consuming and critical phase. It involves:

DELEGATING AND CLEARLY ASSIGNING RESPONSIBILITY FOR SPECIFIC TASKS

This involves building confidence, checking understanding, and coaching, as well as structuring the organization so that people are positioned to achieve their tasks. Critically, the best practice here is to do with communication. Ensure that all those involved know the decision, understand, and support it. This includes people who seem to be on the periphery but are key influencers as their support is essential.

MOTIVATING, MOBILIZING, AND REWARDING THOSE INVOLVED

To ensure that the decision is accomplished to the highest standards, it is important to provide incentives—remuneration, recognition, and status can often mobilize people to succeed.

MANAGING RESOURCES

The people carrying out the plan must have the necessary equipment to complete their task, and be able to address the problem with a level of support commensurate with the problem itself.

APPROACHES TO PROBLEM SOLVING

Solving a problem can be very messy. No matter how much planning and preparation takes place, the process is often confusing, fast moving, and uncertain—it is comforting to think of decision making as a rational, methodical, and ordered process, but the reality is different. Events are not always ordered or clear and the relevant information may be unavailable. It may be impossible to classify, define, specify, and arrive at an effective solution.

The rational approach provides a framework for action, ensuring nothing is omitted, pitfalls are avoided, and best practices applied. The intuitive approach provides the inspiration, insight, and instinct required to explore the best options. To make intuition work, remember that:

- **Instinct and intuition are valuable forms of tacit knowledge.** The mind is continuously processing information subconsciously. Intuition is a form of tacit knowledge, complementing rather than undermining the rational approach to decision making

- **Emotions filter and guide our decisions.** Decisions are guided by our emotions, which act as filters, prioritizing information and provoking a physical response to influences—from laughter to stress. It is important to know how to manage emotion and instinct effectively, as they provide a clear sense of priority, an understanding of intangibles, and determination. While they can be flawed, they can also provide the spark of creativity, the flash of insight, and the strength to pursue the best course

- **Instinct and pattern recognition can provide the key to analysis and creativity.** Effective analysis depends upon seeing the links between various data and then interpreting the patterns. The ability to perceive patterns across issues, data, and subjects is what distinguishes good decision makers from exceptional ones. Instinct brings with it the ability to cross-refer, to see things laterally and from a different perspective, and it brings into play ideas, insights, and experience from a multitude of sources

ASSESSING YOUR PROBLEM-SOLVING SKILLS

By answering the following questions, you will clarify your approach to problem solving. The questions are designed to assess best practices in practical problem-solving techniques, highlighting areas for improvement. While some questions can be answered "wrongly," and so would require some remedial action to be taken, most questions are not simply "black or white."

- Do you first define your objectives when addressing a problem?

- How creative is your thinking when problem solving?

- Do other people help or hinder your problem solving?

- Do you have the necessary information to solve your problems?

- Do you understand how you think about problems?

- Do you generate multiple solutions when problem solving?

- Do you create a list of priorities for any solution?

- Do you monitor strategies to check they don't create further problems?

- Are you confident in your ability to solve problems?

- Do you balance rational and intuitive techniques for problem solving?

- Do you adapt your problem solving to the type of problem?

- Can your solutions be applied repeatedly in the future?

- Are you clear whether a problem will recur?

The next chapter focuses on the issue of risk when making decisions and solving problems. It will enable you to understand and manage risk, as well as embracing uncertainty and risk as an opportunity.

step 4

HANDLING RISKS

66 Take a chance! All life is a chance. The man who goes the furthest is generally the one who is willing to do and dare. 99

DALE CARNEGIE

66 Risk comes from not knowing what you are doing. 99

WARREN BUFFETT

66 There are risks and costs to a program of action. But they are far less than the long-range risks and costs of comfortable inaction. 99

JOHN F. KENNEDY

RISKY BUSINESS

Risk, a necessary and important component of any decision, arises whenever the consequences of an action are unclear and where there is a possibility of both success and failure. When making decisions, it is important to understand the likelihood of failure—it is this information that should guide the choices you make and the methods you use to reach an objective. Techniques for overcoming the fear of risk are discussed in Step 7.

 Risk is reviewed as undesirable: people would rather have a guarantee of success than a chance of failure. But it is also inevitable and, in a world of increasingly complex opportunity, necessary. Consequently, monitoring and managing risk is critical.

Before learning the technical skills for handling risk, one must adopt the right psychological attitude—embracing risk as an opportunity, visualizing success, and understanding that without a chance of failure there would be no chance for success. Risk may indeed be positive, if it inspires due diligence, creativity, and hard work. Only under extreme circumstances when one cannot afford the consequences of failure, or when success is quite unlikely, should risk inspire trepidation. The risks that result from an activity must be acknowledged, accepted, and managed. Moreover, risk is one of the principal considerations in formulating any strategy, and must be properly understood for successful decisions.

USING RATIO ANALYSIS TO UNDERSTAND RISK

Ratio analysis supports the assessment of decisions and the risks they incorporate and enables decisions to be monitored after they have been taken. This prevents inappropriate or damaging decisions, and allows action to be taken if a problem is encountered. The role of ratios is threefold:

1. To analyze.

2. To monitor and measure performance.

3. To facilitate future plans.

When using ratios ask the following questions:

- Which ratios are most appropriate for each part of the business?

- What does the ratio mean?

- How reliable is the data on which the ratio is based?

- What comparisons are desirable in using a ratio?

USING RATIOS FOR BUSINESS DECISIONS

Ratios are used across a wide spectrum of business activities, from marketing or managing people to production. The most significant ratios relate to markets, assets, providers of capital, suppliers, and employees. Examples of ratios in common use in business include:

- **Creditor and debtor days.** Creditor days measure the number of days on average that a company requires to pay its creditors. In contrast, debtor days measure the reverse—the average number of days that it takes for a company to receive payments. Creditor days offer insight into the creditworthiness of a firm that is in debt and not paying its bills within a reasonable (i.e. agreed) period. Debtor days represent a firm's efficiency in collecting monies owed. Creditor days are calculated by dividing the cumulative amount of unpaid suppliers' bills by sales, then multiplying by 365, while debtor days are calculated by dividing the cumulative amount of accounts receivable by sales, again multiplying by 365

- **Profit vulnerability.** The vulnerability of profits to increasing costs can be monitored by dividing fixed expenditure (for example, fixed overhead costs such as premises or salaries) by total expenditure. This identifies where costs are changing and which costs are causing fluctuations in profitability over time. Profit vulnerability ratios are of particular use in handling risk as they are a metric for risks associated with the cost structure

- **Ratios and employees.** Another important area of risk relates to the people involved in a project or organization—to the risk of them leaving or encountering difficulty or simply failing to meet expectations of productivity. Understanding the depth of this risk relies on accurate measures both of productivity and of its importance. Productivity can be measured in a number of ways. Profit per employee is calculated by dividing profit by the number of employees. A more interesting ratio of how much value each employee adds is calculated by dividing sales, less material costs, by the average number of employees. Changing employment costs are another important factor; for example, training expenditure divided by profit gives a measure of the importance of training costs

Just knowing the current situation using ratios is not enough, however, to appreciate the true risks involved. Appreciating risk is about knowing how the situation might change. It is also about adapting your actions to match this situation.

Risks are amplified along "organizational fault lines": where the organization is weak, the chance of failure is most disastrous. Even the threat of uncertainty may cause disruption.

REDUCING RISK . . .

When one cannot afford to take a risk, perhaps because the consequences of failure are too high, the solution is to reduce the level of risk in the decision. This may bring trade-offs—perhaps minimizing the potential gains—but may also create further problems. Although this may seem an uninspiring approach to risk taking, knowing how to minimize risk is necessary to ensure the results of decisions accurately reflect the risk undertaken.

Reducing the risk inherent in business decisions is rarely a linear process. It is, however, always a rational process. Understanding and accepting risk may be intuitive, but risk reduction is rational—best achieved by applying principles and techniques appropriate to the situation.

A framework for risk reduction is outlined below.

UNDERSTAND THE RISKS

> Knowing that every action carries with it certain risks is an essential part of business, as is the principle that the higher the risk, the higher the rate of return needed to justify it.

The willingness to take risks defines entrepreneurship. Interestingly, a 1999 study commissioned by PriceWaterhouseCoopers concluded that in continental Europe strategies are most often oriented toward avoiding and hedging risk, while Anglo-American companies view risk as an opportunity, consciously accepting the responsibility of risk management as necessary to achieving their goals.

Successful decision makers understand this, taking steps to ensure risks are measured, the likely consequences are understood, and risks only ever mitigated when the consequences of failure are too large to be justified by the greatest potential success. Of course, hedging risks is good practice, ensuring that needless risks are eliminated. Another best practice is to broadly understand all of the risks, rather than focusing on a narrow range. This allows the implementation of risk management procedures that do not ignore important factors, or cause conflicts between organizational objectives. Risks that are avoidable are identified and eliminated, while the impact of others may be curtailed.

Decision makers who follow this approach take a holistic view of risk: moving beyond the direct financial perspective and actively managing risk as it affects the whole organization. This means measuring risks and clearly understanding all the potential consequences and their danger signals, to give early warning of failure while there is still a chance to do something. Accepting that risks exist provides a starting point: the pressing need then becomes, in most organizations, to create the right climate for risk management. People need to understand the reasons for control systems, necessitating good communication and leadership.

CONSIDER THE AMOUNT OF RISK

 Once the risks have been identified, the next step is to consider whether the risks are worth it.

There are two factors to consider when assessing whether to take a risk. One is the risk appetite, and the risk-bearing capacity, of the organization—i.e. the level of risk that is acceptable given the decision. It is best to be clear about this from the start: articulate the nature and extent of the risks that are acceptable. The other factor is the level of risk that is being incurred. This is directly proportional to the negative effects of the risk and to the probability of the risks becoming reality. Then, you may see whether the risks are worth it—if so, the decision should go ahead. Nevertheless, it is still worth considering how you can reduce the risks further.

IDENTIFY AND PRIORITIZE RISKS

 Always account for the human dimension. People behave differently, perhaps inconsistently and frequently irrationally when making decisions involving risk.

People's behavior when confronted with risk may derive from a lack of understanding about the need for risk and the fact that it is inevitable. It may derive from a pervasive overconfidence—refusing to admit a chance of failure. Or, they may simply overlook some of the key risks. Risk should inform every decision and everyone in the organization must understand this to minimize the damage the risks may cause. Nobody reacts well to unnecessary surprises. Removing the "surprise" factor is one important way of reducing the impact of certain risks.

When mitigating risks, start by reducing or eliminating those that result only in cost—the non-trading risks. These include property damage risks, legal and contractual liabilities, and business interruption risks, and can be thought of as the "fixed costs" of risk. Reduce these risks with techniques such as quality assurance programs, environmental control processes, enforcement of employee health and safety regulations, installation of accident prevention and emergency equipment and training, and security to prevent crime, sabotage, espionage, and threats to people and systems. These are "reactive" measures. And reducing the risk will reduce the cost of insuring or hedging against it!

Risk surrounds us all of the time. Former British Prime Minister Harold Macmillan declared that "to be alive at all involves some risk." The most common areas of risk must be understood: they lie in every area of an organization's operations. When attempting to identify risks, defining the categories into which they fall will allow for a more structured analysis, reducing the chances of risks being overlooked. And along with the endless lists of tangible risks can be added another, intangible category. This is the opportunity cost associated with risk, as avoiding a risk may mean avoiding a potentially huge opportunity. The greatest risk of all could be to do nothing.

. . . OR MANAGING RISK

When it is accepted that risk is inevitable (and desirable if associated with greater opportunities), then it is time to manage the risk.

Poor risk management may lead to undue harm and decisions coming unstuck. Risk management is mostly a game of perception: your understanding is the key to competence. How you perceive risks determines your attitude to them and, in turn, your success. Understanding risk, the argument goes, requires an understanding of the *catalysts* that cause risks to be realized. Risk is simply a probability. Manipulating this probability is the essence of risk management: removing these catalysts will remove the risk.

Once risks are identified they can be prioritized according to both their potential impact and their probability, to highlight not only where things might go wrong, but also how, why, and where the catalysts might be triggered.

So, what are the five most significant catalysts today?

TECHNOLOGY

New hardware, software, or system configuration can trigger risks, as can new demands placed on existing information systems and technology. As so many critical systems in business depend on technology, any technological problems can be extremely disruptive. Technological change also places stress on employees (who have to adapt and learn) and customers and suppliers (who may have to adjust their relationship with the business). It carries no guarantees of success. Most new technologies promise great benefits to business, but it is important not to forget how they might damage, disrupt, and cost the organization.

ORGANIZATIONAL CHANGE

Risks are triggered by issues such as new management structures or reporting lines, new strategies, and new commercial agreements (such as mergers or distribution agreements). The complexity of this risk is illustrated by British retailer Marks & Spencer's expansion into overseas markets. This was a new and challenging strategy for the long-established business. Unhappily for its managers and shareholders, the strategy failed to deliver the anticipated results and when this was combined with pressures in its core markets

71

significant measures were needed to get the firm back on track. Brand change is notoriously difficult to execute, as the familiar is always a safer resting place than the unknown! Changing approaches to managing people carries the risk of deteriorating employee relations, either because of inexperience in the new approaches, or the ensuing climate of uncertainty.

PROCESSES

New products, markets, and acquisitions precipitate process change, triggering risks. People can use the methods they know better than they can use alternative methods—even if the other methods are easier! And new processes may not, despite their allure, be right for the situation—Daimler-Benz's thorough and efficient processes were not suitable for Chrysler's creative, "freewheeling" processes used successfully in the American car market, as they found out when the two companies merged in 1998. The disastrous launch of "New Coke" by Coca-Cola was met by an outraged population of cola drinkers and non-drinkers alike, who felt angry that their iconic American product was being changed. This product launch was a bigger risk than anyone at the firm had realized. The firm's ability to turn the situation to their advantage showed that risk can be managed and controlled, but such success is rare and only open to the strongest brands.

PEOPLE

New personnel, a loss of key people, poor succession planning, or poor people management can all lead to dislocation. However, the main cause of dislocation within this category is behavior: everything from laziness to fraud, exhaustion to simple human error can all be catalysts resulting in risk being realized. This situation is most obviously demonstrated by the massive financial scandal that shook Barings Bank in Singapore during the mid-1990s, resulting from the actions of one rogue trader.

EXTERNAL ENVIRONMENTAL FACTORS

Changes such as regulatory, political, economic, or social developments all severely affect strategic decisions, bringing to the surface risks that may have lain hidden. For example, the sudden and tragic arrival of the SARS epidemic in Asia in 2003 significantly affected economic confidence and performance throughout the region. This risk could not have been foreseen.

STAGES IN RISK MANAGEMENT

The stages of managing the risk inherent in decisions are simple:

1. Assess and analyze the risks resulting from the decision through a systematic process of risk identification and, ideally, quantification.

2. Consider how best to avoid or mitigate risks.

3. In parallel with the second stage, take action to manage, control, and monitor the risks.

ASSESSING AND MINIMIZING RISKS

It is harder to assess the risks inherent in a business decision than to identify them.

Risks that precipitate losses, such as employee-related problems or difficulties with suppliers, may be understood with the help of past experience. Unusual losses are harder to quantify. Risks with little likelihood of occurring in the next five years do not hold much meaning for a company trying to meet shareholders' immediate expectations. As each risk may have a different level of impact, it is essential to quantify the potential consequences of identified risks, and then define courses of action to mitigate or remove them. Risks can be categorized in terms of both likely frequency and potential impact. Moreover, the potential consequences of risk may be ranked on a scale ranging from inconvenient to catastrophic.

Experience repeatedly shows that risk has to be actively managed and accorded a high priority—not only within the decision-making process but permanently and across the organization as a whole. This might mean that risk management procedures and techniques are well documented, clearly communicated, regularly reviewed, and monitored. To manage risks, you must know what they are, what factors affect them, and what the impact may be. By plotting the ability to control the risk against its potential impact, as shown in the figure below, you may decide either to exercise greater control, or to mitigate the potential impact. Risks falling into the top right quadrant are the priorities for action. Nevertheless, the bottom right quadrant (total/significant control, major/critical impact) should not be ignored as management complacency, mistakes, and a lack of control can lead to the risk being realized.

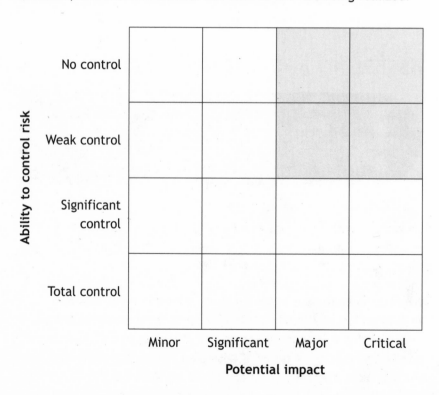

MINIMIZING THE THREAT FROM RISK

Once the risks have been prioritized and assessed, they can be reduced or mitigated with simple techniques such as sharing them with a partner, monitoring, or subjecting them to contingency plans. For example, acceptable service level agreements from vendors are essential to reduce risk. Joint ventures, licensing, and agency agreements are also different ways of mitigating risk.

To minimize the chances of things going wrong, it is important to focus on the quality of what people do: doing the right things right reduces risks and costs. Actively managing and using information is crucial. The ethos of an organization should recognize and reward behavior that manages risk. This requires a commitment by senior managers and the resources (which include training) to match.

A survey by PriceWaterhouseCoopers of 100 American companies with revenues between $250 million and $30 billion revealed that more than half of their managers believed controls got in the way of getting work done. Rather than seeing risk management as an integral part of business that could assist firms in achieving their corporate objectives, it was viewed as a bureaucratic burden and policing process. In short, it seems that control systems are often seen as getting in the way of people doing their jobs, rather than things that help make sure they don't do their jobs badly. So risk aversion still predominates in business.

Everyone accepts that risks need to be taken if you are to keep ahead of the competition. The answer seems to be a better understanding of what the real risks are, for people to genuinely share responsibility for the risks being taken, and for people to change their own mindset, embracing risk as an opportunity, not a threat.

The conventional approach to managing risk is not the only strategy. Another approach is to look for ways to make progress by using the risk to achieve success, either by adding value or by outstripping competitors—or both. To do this, organizations need to stop taking the fun out of risk, to stop controlling it in a way that is often perceived as bureaucratic and stifling. As any entrepreneur will tell you, risk is both desirable, providing new opportunities to learn, develop, and move forward, and necessary, compelling people to improve and effectively meet the current of challenge and change.

AUDITING YOUR APPROACH TO RISK

By answering the following questions, you will clarify your personal approach to handling risk. The questions are designed to assess your grasp of best practices in handling risk as well as to identify your personal approach to risk, highlighting any areas for improvement. While some questions can be answered "wrongly," demanding remedial action, most questions are not "black and white."

Rate each question on a scale from 1 to 5, where:

1 = never

2 = seldom

3 = sometimes

4 = often

5 = always

Your risks	1	2	3	4	5
1. Do you approach risk by first analyzing it and measuring it, before taking any decision?					
2. Are risks prevented from evolving into problems?					
3. Are people encouraged to view certain risks as opportunities?					
4. Do people fully realize the potential consequences of their actions, and are they equipped to understand, avoid, control, or mitigate risk?					
5. Do you take responsibility for risks and the decisions that go with them, rather than passing it onto others?					
6. Are the risks inherent in strategic decisions (e.g. acquiring a new business or entering a new market) adequately understood?					
7. Do you identify all the areas of risk relating to your decisions?					
8. Do you list all the disruptive events that could prove damaging?					
9. Is risk actively monitored?					
10. Do you react calmly to the pressures risk creates?					
11. Do you ensure that no unacceptable risk is taken?					
12. Do you and those around you actively minimize the organization's overall exposure to risk?					
13. Do you react to risk with hard work, diligence, and entrepreneurship?					
Total:					

A score of 45 or more indicates that you appreciate risk management and understand the main risks you face, and react soundly, confidently, and prudently to them in practice as well as "in theory."

Scores between 35 and 45 show a clear tendency to deal with risk rationally and in a conscientious manner. However, the risk management process could be improved by removing certain risks or by developing an environment around you that can better deal with any problems that might evolve out of the risks. Go over the rational aspects of the process to see if you have any weaknesses, while retaining the confidence to embrace risk and see it as an opportunity for success. Be careful, however—high scores can indicate an overconfidence in your approach to risk.

Scores of less than 35 suggest that your risk management approach is too haphazard. There are, almost certainly, factors obstructing the problem-solving process. Also, the negative reaction to risk will create more problems than there were in the first place!

One essential element in any decision—but particularly those that are complex, long-lasting, or part of a larger process—is the need to use the right information in the right way at the right time. As we have seen, information is an important aspect of most decisions and solutions, affecting such issues as managing risk. The next chapter:

- Sets out the main benefits of managing knowledge and information

- Describes how to prepare for decision making by establishing an effective information management framework

- Demonstrates the importance of good information management in effective problem solving and decision making

- Develops your understanding of core concepts surrounding knowledge and information

- Clarifies why a clear understanding of these concepts will lead to effective decision making and problem solving

- Improves your techniques for using information and helps ensure that your learning directly improves your decision making and problem solving

- Promotes thoughtful, accurate decisions and solutions grounded in reality

USING THE RIGHT INFORMATION AND KNOWLEDGE

"I find more and more executives less and less well-informed about the outside world, if only because they believe that the data on the computer printouts are ipso facto information . . . We live in an economy where knowledge, not buildings and machinery, is the chief resource and where knowledge-workers make up the biggest part of the workforce. Until well into the 20th century, most workers were manual workers. Today . . . 40% of our total work force, are knowledge-workers."

PETER DRUCKER

"I came to see that an objective view of the facts was one of the most important aspects of successful management. People go wrong most often when their decisions are based upon inadequate knowledge of the facts available."

HAROLD GENEEN, FORMER CHAIRMAN OF ITT

MANAGING KNOWLEDGE

Knowledge is the stock of factual data and understanding about the "real world" possessed by an individual: it is far more than pure data. Knowledge represents the experience and expertise found within an organization. Arguably, it is the scarcest resource.

This chapter explains how knowledge can be used better and why it should not be allowed to become outdated. The chapter also highlights the consequences of information failure and equips you with the techniques to avoid this, making knowledge and information your allies when making decisions or solving problems.

Information and knowledge share similarities, and what is particularly important is that they be actively recognized, controlled, and managed before, during, and after the decision-making process.

Information is usually regarded as objective, whereas knowledge includes elements of interpretation and understanding. This is the key to using knowledge effectively: it is how we use our knowledge to solve problems and inform decisions that we are judged on. Make no mistake, knowledge is essential for making successful decisions and solving problems quickly and reliably. A poor use of knowledge is more than just waste: it is the most frequented path to failure.

Developments in technology have allowed an explosion in the scope and depth of the knowledge accessible to the decision maker or problem solver. Currently, what defines successful organizations is the ability to deploy this vast information resource creatively, ensuring that it assists strategy without confining it to mere figures with no intuitive understanding. The tension between these two extremes leads organizations and individuals astray. Scarce or poorly managed information and knowledge may precipitate suspicion, frustration, or resentment—creating additional problems and obstructing the future flow of information and knowledge. Furthermore, introducing systems to control information can be disruptive, causing pressure and demanding investment in both time and capital.

AN EXAMPLE OF THE SIGNIFICANCE OF INFORMATION FOR DECISION MAKING: THE CUBAN MISSILE CRISIS

The need to constantly and methodically question information was highlighted by the 1962 Cuban Missile Crisis. With the Soviet Union installing nuclear weapons 90 miles from mainland America, prompting an American naval blockade of Cuba, the two superpowers were at a dangerous impasse. Finally, after a tense standoff, President Kennedy received a communication from the Soviet leader, Khrushchev, saying that he would agree to remove their weapons. However, this was followed up within hours by another message saying that Soviet withdrawal was conditional on America removing nuclear weapons from bases in Turkey—terms unacceptable to the Americans.

Kennedy paused and questioned the information, then decided to ignore the second message and quickly wrote back to Khrushchev acknowledging that America recognized and accepted the first letter. Although Kennedy did not know it at the time, *the second message was sent first*. One of the lasting outcomes of the Cuban Missile Crisis was the establishment of a "hotline"—a direct telephone link between the leaders of the two countries to prevent such a potentially disastrous misunderstanding.

KNOWLEDGE, INFORMATION, AND DECISION MAKING

Knowledge is the intellectual capital an organization possesses. This capitalizes on the broad wealth of experience and expertise within an organization.

There is increasing recognition of the benefits of using all the available knowledge to complete tasks, ignoring nothing, and taking a wide definition of "relevant previous experience." With mostly positive consequences, this means that knowledge and information are critical resources for decision making. It is a clear asset to possess an effective system that allows information and expertise to flow freely to key points in the organization for use by those who need it.

Information has a number of aspects, positive and negative, that impact on the decision-making process. It can:

- Affect people's judgment and behavior. Information management may cause suspicion, frustration, or resentment if it is withheld or ineffectively deployed

- Change the way people act, their responsibilities and the work that they do. It has a major effect on status, training needs, accountability, and level of control and determines how they delegate, manage time, recruit, communicate, and lead, as well as make decisions

- Produce disruptive short-term upheavals, creating additional pressure

Success hinges on understanding, planning, and controlling the organization's flow of information—as well as the expertise (or knowledge) that is contained within the business—so that it supports decision making. It also hinges on everyone appreciating the immense value of knowledge.

TECHNIQUES FOR MANAGING KNOWLEDGE

Here is a paradox: the knowledge and information that should improve decisions and solutions put such a stress on organizations as to confuse, disrupt, and deter people from using these resources or, at the least, they give false impressions. Avoiding this is the focus of knowledge management.

There are many techniques for acquiring information including surveys, telephone calls, meetings, and interviews, along with other sources such as libraries and information centers, all providing insight. Online sources provide a valuable source of regularly updated information. The appropriate technique depends on the nature of the decision. By reviewing and analyzing information, viable options emerge.

> Decisions are about human judgment. Nevertheless, quantitative methods highlight trends and anomalies, and careful analysis will improve everyone's understanding.

Information must be widely accessible, clearly labeled, categorized, relevant, and up to date. As if this were not enough, the system and processes for storing and retrieving information need to be cost effective.

Several techniques for effective knowledge management are outlined below.

UNDERTAKE A KNOWLEDGE AUDIT

Few firms appreciate what knowledge they possess—often because knowledge is confined to a few, tucked away in inaccessible places or simply neglected as an issue. Everyone in the organization should uncover this hidden knowledge, akin to finding buried treasure.

A knowledge audit is designed to uncover the breadth, depth, and location of an organization's knowledge, in three stages:

1. **Defining** what knowledge assets exist—especially the information or skills that would be difficult or expensive to replace.

2. **Locating** those assets: who keeps or "owns" them.

3. **Classifying** them and assessing how they relate to other assets. In this way, opportunities can be found in other parts of the organization.

INCREASE KNOWLEDGE

After a knowledge audit, the next stage is to use the results to develop knowledge and information that support the decisions and problems that must be addressed. The knowledge audit will show where knowledge is lacking—highlighting areas where it must be increased. The challenge becomes increasing the knowledge base, which can be done in three main ways:

1. **Buying**—for example, by hiring staff, forming alliances and partnerships, outsourcing, and purchasing intelligence (such as industry reports).

2. **Renting**—for example, by hiring consultants or subcontracting work to meet the needs of a situation where you alone do not have the resources.

3. **Developing**—for example, through training and continuous learning, which organically add to the organization's knowledge over time.

MAINTAIN KNOWLEDGE

Knowledge gaps make an organization more vulnerable to competition. The "downsizing" (or redundancy) strategies that many firms have followed have highlighted the dangers of getting rid of people with expertise and experience, in pursuit of short-term cost savings. Short-term finance is often a less decisive resource than the knowledge and expertise it is traded for, and such downsizing often leaves organizations ill-equipped to cope with problems and make reliable decisions. Added to this, and as we described in Step 1, traditional employee loyalty has become significantly eroded and it is therefore important to capture, classify, and store people's expertise and tacit knowledge.

PROTECT KNOWLEDGE

Since knowledge produces competitive advantage, it must be protected. This requires an understanding of knowledge, which falls into two categories: *explicit* and *tacit*.

Examples of explicit knowledge include copyright or information codified in handbooks, systems, or procedures. Tacit knowledge is knowledge that is retained by individuals, including learning, experience, observation, deduction, and informally acquired knowledge. Explicit knowledge can be protected through legal procedures, and although tacit knowledge can to some extent be protected by legal methods (such as non-compete clauses in employment contracts) this is usually unsatisfactory. It is sensible to ensure that valuable tacit knowledge is recorded and passed on to others before it is lost. While explicit knowledge usually represents an obvious form of expense (such as the research required to obtain a patent), tacit knowledge is no less valuable.

FORMALIZE INFORMATION SYSTEMS

An efficient information management system will not just coordinate and control information, it will enable new information to be integrated with the existing stock of information. This ensures one's understanding draws on all resources. When developing a system, decide what information is needed, even preparing a "wish list" of what will help improve decisions and achieve objectives. Assimilating new information in an ad hoc and disorganized way appeals as an easy way to store information—but where is the knowledge? Formalizing stocks of information enables it to be recalled conveniently and disseminated accurately. Consequently, your information will become more active and useful in decision making and problem solving. Too much data can only confuse. Knowing who requires each item of information involves assessing how information flows through an organization.

Often, information flows according to status—from the top to the bottom. Whether this is always desirable is highly questionable.

HARNESSING THE INFORMATION LIFE CYCLE

An important concept when dealing with knowledge and information is the concept of flow: how new information is assimilated into the existing base of understanding. This is termed the *information life cycle*—from birth to death, information must be viewed organically. Success in decision making and problem solving can hinge on understanding how information flows, what it is used for, and the ways in which it is applied.

Information can be viewed as going through a cycle, as follows:

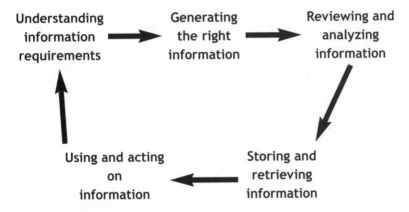

The stages in which information is used may blend into each other, but in organizing the flow of information it helps to think in terms of separate stages, each with its own characteristics and techniques.

UNDERSTANDING INFORMATION REQUIREMENTS

Knowing what information is needed is a prerequisite to ensuring its availability and reliability. It is often worth asking colleagues and subordinates key questions about their information requirements. These include what information is needed, how it should be presented, when it needs to be supplied, where it comes from, what restrictions there are on the information, and which decisions and problems it is relevant to.

GENERATING THE RIGHT INFORMATION

Understanding what information is needed is one thing; getting it is entirely another matter. The key is to approach the task in two ways: acquiring the information and verifying it. Techniques to consider when seeking and acquiring information vary according to the type of information needed. Some popular approaches to generating data include:

- Traditional desk research methods (for example, questionnaires, surveys, telephone calls, meetings, and interviews) and online sources (not only the Internet, but also companies selling information services, such as Reuters)

- Asking people who have experienced a similar situation can be very useful, if only for building confidence. Asking people who have never encountered the situation before can also help as it provides a fresh objectivity to the situation

Of course, the best approach depends entirely on the nature of the decision to be made. Networking is essential for generating data and has gained in popularity and acceptance with the realization that helping others can also mean helping oneself.

REVIEWING AND ANALYZING INFORMATION

Analyzing information is an entire discipline in itself, with many quantitative methods that help in making sense of information, highlighting trends as well as anomalies. The process of reviewing and analyzing information is invariably the starting point for solving the problem or finding the best decision. The reviewing process not only enables possible options to emerge, but can also be used to scrutinize them and rate their effectiveness.

There are many rules and standards to ensure the full and proper analysis of information, but the guiding principle must be to maintain objectivity so that the decision is fair, logical, and practical. This is particularly important for complex decisions. However, using information to justify a predetermined course of action is a waste of time. If you have already made your decision, then it is surely better to spend one's energies taking action than to look for some justification that may or may not exist.

Challenging the information—asking why something is the way it appears—is an important step in analyzing the information, formulating ideas, removing assumptions, and generating practical, workable solutions. Also, once information has been generated, it is possible to move beyond quantitative and statistical analysis, with scenario-planning, modeling, and simulation. The key is to try to create a realistic set of circumstances and account for as many variables as possible.

STORING AND RETRIEVING INFORMATION

This stage of the information life cycle is difficult to balance: it is often either totally overlooked or made the most important aspect of information management. Information should not form a mountain and neither should it be select or, worse, entirely absent. The following elements are important when storing and retrieving information for decision making:

- Accessibility at the point of use

- Its labeling and categorization

- Its relevance

- Its cost: expensive, cumbersome information systems help no one

USING AND ACTING ON INFORMATION

The final stage of the information life cycle involves using the information to generate ideas, formulate plans, reach conclusions, and make the decision. This stage is what makes the information worthwhile; without it, there is no point in having the information in the first place. This last stage pulls together the rest of the process, and as the decision is implemented the cycle starts over again, with additional information requirements being identified. Only when trying to act on the existing facts can the need for new facts be properly understood!

In conclusion, monitoring decisions after they have been made is important. This will help assess whether new decisions are necessary, and whether the information for future choices needs to change. Adherence to a methodical framework as the decision is made or the solution applied may help overcome the chaotic aspects of this stage that can cause so much confusion. Information needs to be used as a tool and managed objectively throughout the decision-making process. Often this is difficult to sustain, but the danger is that decisions taken during the final implementation will be wrong, undermining the final outcome. Finally, it is important to manage time constraints and deal proactively with any pressures that may exist. Certain situations require fast decisions, but the key is not to be bullied by information. The information life cycle exists so that you are in control of the information; the information is your ally.

USING YOUR KNOWLEDGE WHEN MAKING DECISIONS

Given the many billions of dollars invested each year in IT software and hardware, one would expect managers to know exactly how information technology improves their organization's performance, and how to control information to improve effectiveness. However, research indicates that managers are largely unaware of what they need to do to ensure that investments in information and knowledge deliver bottom line improvements in performance. In other words, information is gathered, stored, and maintained—at exorbitant expense—but not put to use. The same applies for softer forms of information. How often do people utilize all of their personal experiences to inform their decisions and resolve problems?

In research conducted at IMD Business School, Professor Donald Marchand, together with William J. Kettinger, identified three critical factors driving successful information use, which combine to provide an overall measure of *Information Orientation* (IO). Since you cannot manage the invisible, they argue that using information and knowledge effectively demands accurately measuring it, in all its forms rather than just in terms of data. Unfortunately, many managers see the use of information only within the narrow context of technology, yet this alone cannot yield sustainable competitive advantage.

Statistical research involving over 1,000 senior managers from 98 companies in 22 countries demonstrated the existence of three information capabilities:

1. **Information behaviors and values.** This is the capability of an organization to instill and promote behavior that leads to the effective use of information. Managers should promote integrity, formality, control, transparency, and sharing, as well as removing barriers to information flow and promoting information use.

2. **Information management practices.** Managing information involves sensing, collecting, organizing, processing, and maintaining information. Managers set up processes, train their employees, and take responsibility for the management of information. This focuses their organizations on the right information. They must minimize the hazard of information overload, improve the quality of information available to employees, and use this to enhance decision making.

3. **Information technology practices.** IT applications and infrastructure should support decision making. Consequently, business strategy needs to be linked to IT strategy so that the infrastructure supports operations, business processes, innovation, and decisions.

No matter what the scale, building these capabilities will improve how information and knowledge is actively used. This will improve decision making and problem solving. However, do not forget that information can only assist people: the human factor remains critical. People must use the information and systems, share their knowledge with others, and move beyond existing knowledge to innovate.

Improving the quality of the decisions we make and solving problems in ever better ways is a game of ideas. Decisions and problems can be attacked through flashes of creative brilliance, but whatever their source, new ideas are the essence of improvement. Ideas are central to making the right decisions, solving problems, and adding value for customers. And new ideas must derive from a base of knowledge; the way organizations and individuals use information and knowledge to improve themselves and their situation is the process of learning.

IMPROVING DECISIONS WITH ORGANIZATIONAL LEARNING

The well-used term "organizational learning" applies equally well to individual people—it simply refers to the application and use of knowledge. The common definition of the "learning organization" is:

> **66An organization skilled at creating, acquiring, and transferring knowledge, and at modifying its behavior to reflect new knowledge and insights.99**

It is this last part of the definition—the need to modify behavior—where so many organizations fail. It is not the information that fails, but how one reacts to this information and uses it.

The learning process can be viewed in four stages: real world experiences, reflective observation, abstract conceptualization, and active experimentation. This is a useful conceptual framework for how one learns; mastery of these stages is a good platform for success.

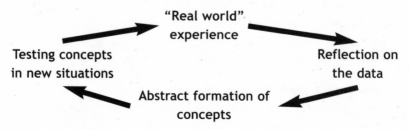

94

- Learning begins with *observing* what has occurred, reflecting on what has been observed, and assessing the underlying structures that drive the behavior we observed

- This provides knowledge of the situation being faced. From this, we *develop a theory* as to what is happening, which influences the development of a decision. However, reality will invariably deviate from the theory, drawing our attention to what is different from our expectation and thus demanding that we modify our understanding. This initiates the next iteration of the learning cycle, with reflection, conceptualization, and mental model building

- This learning is a continuous process. Reflection and action are the two sides of learning: without action there can be no learning, as all that one can then reflect on is one's previous reflections

Organizational learning occurs when the learning cycle is performed collectively in the organization. This is when people reflect on their experiences, collectively developing new theories based on observation, and then acting together. In the process of joint reflection, there is a sharing of individual views leading to a shared understanding. However, most people dislike abstract reflection, preferring to focus on action—"doing" rather than thinking and discussing. Perhaps this derives from narrowly designed reward systems in organizations that encourage only a few activities. Either way, business decisions fail and problems linger too often because of managers' inability, or lack of willingness, to pause and reflect.

The following techniques will improve how both you and your organization approach learning:

- **Foster an atmosphere conducive to learning.** Give managers time to pause and reflect, use their knowledge to generate new insights and ideas, and, above all, to learn. This process may be obstructed by pressure or stress

- **Stimulate the exchange of ideas.** This is often best done by reducing bureaucracy and boundaries; most organizations fail because their structures, hierarchies, and boundaries inhibit the flow of information. This isolates critical individuals and reinforces the power of personal myths and generalizations. Emphasizing communication and opening up the organization leads to a fresh flow of ideas, competing perspectives, and insights. Jack Welch, former CEO of General Electric, views "boundarylessness" as one of the most potent forces for change

- **Create learning forums.** When working within a supportive, stimulating environment, people naturally foster learning, enabling them to work with new knowledge and to consider its implications. A learning forum can be any opportunity ranging from a strategic review or benchmark report to a visit to customers

These steps are just a start. Actions that remove barriers to learning (for example, using appraisals to engender support and enthusiasm for learning) will result in improved decisions and actions by promoting better knowledge and understanding.

AUDIT YOUR USE OF KNOWLEDGE AND INFORMATION

By answering the following questions, you will clarify your personal approach to using information and knowledge to improve your decision making and problem solving. Also, it will highlight the areas where you need to improve your use of knowledge and information. While some questions can be answered "wrongly," demanding remedial action, most questions are not "black and white." Rate each question on a scale from 1 to 5, where: 1 is never, 2 is seldom, 3 is sometimes, 4 is often, 5 is always.

Auditing your knowledge and understanding	1	2	3	4	5
1. Consider a specific task and ask do you understand what information and knowledge is needed?					
2. Is your information and knowledge presented in a way that facilitates the task?					
3. Is your information and knowledge available when it is needed, to those who need it?					
4. Are you aware of all the decisions and problems that your information could improve?					
5. Do you undertake a knowledge audit before the decision-making or problem-solving process?					
6. Do you ensure that, rather than just collate data, you have actively useful information?					
7. Do you use technology to positively influence your decision making and problem solving (e.g. for managing or innovating)?					
8. Does information flow freely and easily through your organization to those that need it?					
9. Are you aware of the source of the information and issues concerning its reliability?					
10. Is information used in your organization proactively?					
11. Is your information transparent, controlled, and appropriately formalized, with its veracity and integrity protected?					
Total:					

A score of 45 or more indicates that you appreciate the many uses of information and knowledge, make informed decisions, and solve problems accurately and sustainably. Areas for improvement are, most likely, outside the area of managing information—competency here does not preclude weaknesses in other areas, so failure may still come.

Scores between 30 and 45 show a clear tendency to deal with information rationally and proactively, combined with an intuitive understanding of its uses and of the situation in which you are working. However, the information management process could be improved by removing certain obstacles, or by capitalizing on information and knowledge that is currently languishing. Go over the rational aspects of the process to see if you have any weaknesses, while ensuring that excessive formality doesn't shut down certain types of knowledge—or bar critical people from what they need. A word of caution: high scores can indicate overconfidence, perhaps because of a lack of appreciation of all the types of information and knowledge available.

Scores of less than 30 suggest that your approach to dealing with knowledge and information is too haphazard, that you do not fully understand or apply it to your decisions and problems and that, generally, your decisions are undermined and problems amplified by a lack of skills in this area. Perhaps you make the mistake of disregarding your *knowledge base*: what is known and how you can use it. A bad habit in the twenty-first century is simply to rely on technology and organizational processes, taking little responsibility for learning yourself. Consequently, the whole situation becomes dehumanized and the wealth of knowledge that individuals possess is disregarded—leading to failure.

Decisions come in a variety of sizes and guises, yet because they are invariably linked together in a complex web by factors such as perception, cause, effect, and precedent, they *all* need to be actively understood and controlled. The next chapter provides an overview of the main types of decision (urgent, routine, long-term, simple but vital, and complex decisions). The characteristics of each type of decision are outlined, but perhaps more importantly, practical techniques for handling different decisions are explained.

step **6**

HANDLING DIFFERENT
TYPES OF DECISION

> **An expert problem solver must be endowed with two incompatible qualities—a restless imagination and a patient pertinacity.**
>
> HOWARD W. EVES

> **The easy way out usually leads back in.**
>
> PETER SENGE

HANDLING URGENT DECISIONS

Decisions may seem urgent, and people may say that they are critical and time-sensitive, but this does not always mean that they actually are urgent. It is easy to believe that a particular decision needs to be made quickly, especially if other people are waiting for a choice to be made or a course of action set, or if there is a great deal of work to be done and decisions made. Urgent decisions are often simply a matter of perception: one person's urgent decision is another person's routine choice.

Urgent decisions clearly do exist and they need to be both recognized and approached methodically.

Significant decisions are rarely straightforward and other factors may well need to be set against the urgency of the decision. These include:

- The likelihood of success

- The potential risks resulting from failure

- The need to wait for the outcome of other decisions

- The priority of the decision relative to other work

- The resources available

These are the main factors although many other issues can influence how urgent decisions are perceived and approached. Techniques for handling urgent decisions are outlined below.

UNDERSTAND WHY THE DECISION IS URGENT AND WHAT IS INVOLVED

Urgent decisions need to be clearly understood and the essential aspects must be carefully assessed, but there is always a danger in oversimplifying any decision. Instead, understand the background and take as long as possible to research and analyze.

If urgent decisions keep recurring in one area, or if they can be anticipated, then the best approach is to prepare systems in advance so that they are ready to provide any necessary information. This is particularly the case in crisis management, for example, and many organizations have resources (notably teams and procedures) prepared in advance should a crisis arise.

MANAGE TIME EFFICIENTLY

When tackling urgent decisions it is important to understand how much time is available, and then to use it to the full. Techniques that can help include:

- **Avoid getting distracted with other people's problems.** This means being polite but firm and saying no when needed

- **Ask for help or support.** It may be that people do not understand the urgency of your situation—if they did they would be quite willing to help

- **Delegate appropriate tasks** to others wherever possible as this will free up some of your time. It is important, though, to match person to task, and to be clear about what you want done, how it will be accomplished, and how and when you will monitor the work

- **Prioritize.** Faced with a complex mass of urgent tasks it can be difficult to know where to start; assessing and ranking priorities can help. If this is not feasible, then an alternative is to see whether the decision breaks down into a linear sequence of events with an obvious starting point or first task. If that fails, then my personal preference is to start with aspects of the task that are relatively small and get them out of the way, building momentum for the process as a whole

- **Manage your environment,** for example by removing distractions and taking time for you to improve your own chances of success. If the urgent decisions are flowing steadily, as in a crisis situation, then the key is to take time to recharge and reinvigorate yourself whenever possible

USE SKILLS OF ASSERTION

During any decision-making process interruptions and distractions arise all the time; the problem when they arise during urgent decisions is that they will be unwelcome and distracting. The key is to keep in mind the need to make and implement the priority decision, and explain to people clearly, politely, but firmly what your priority is. If you avoid doing this, then there is the chance of misunderstanding, even resentment, arising.

IGNORE TRIVIA

The really important point here is to stay focused on the key issues relevant to the urgent decision, rather than getting sidetracked into ancillary decisions that are unrelated and can wait. The research, analysis, and implementation phases of the decision-making process are fundamental here, as they will clearly highlight those issues that are central to the matter in hand and those that can be ignored.

FOLLOW THE DECISION-MAKING PROCESS

The decision-making process may seem lengthy and the tendency may be to avoid it altogether in preference for an intuitive, "quick fix" solution, but this ignores the element of risk that makes a decision urgent in the first place. Time constraints and significance combine to make decisions urgent; however, if you follow the correct process (see p. 19) then you increase the chances of making the right choice and making it work in the time available. In urgent circumstances the original six-stage process can be adapted to:

1. **Defining and agreeing the objective.** It may be necessary simply to define the objective and seek agreement for the process as a whole later.

2. **Researching, analyzing, and understanding relevant information.** Understanding and analysis are essential: without them the process of decision making is reduced largely to guesswork. However, background research and detailed understanding will need to be avoided: simply grasp the essentials.

3. **Devising ideas and options.** Preparation in advance can help, as can other short-cuts such as brainstorming or seeking the views of others outside the situation who can provide a different approach, or much-needed objectivity and clarity. This stage often needs to be conducted together with the evaluation phase. Each option is devised and considered; it is then either rejected or held in reserve while a better option is sought. If no better option is found, then the solution is at hand.

4. **Implementing the decision.** This stage needs to be combined with monitoring the effects, so that each step in the process of implementation takes into account what is happening and actions are adjusted accordingly.

STAY FOCUSED UNTIL THE END

It is often easy to focus on selecting the decision—the best course of action—and then failing to follow through on its actual implementation. This is particularly true in the frequently pressurized environment in which urgent decisions are made. The solution is to stay calm and consider the implementation right from the start. It is necessary to understand that a decision is frequently useless unless it is actually applied—a fact that is often the first casualty of urgency!

ENSURING THE SUCCESS OF ROUTINE DECISIONS

Urgent decisions share with long-term decisions the highest profile, usually because they involve other people. However, for the majority of people, urgent and long-term decisions are both relatively infrequent; much more common are the regular, routine decisions taken every day. Although these lack the excitement, profile, and importance of other types of decision, making them work well is, surprisingly, even more important.

Routine decisions are tortoises: they don't look much and they can even be dreary, but they tend to be the ones that gradually make progress and deliver success over time. (High-profile decisions, of course, are hares: their value is usually over-hyped, they are full of flaws, and it is much harder to meet people's inflated expectations!)

POTENTIAL PITFALLS OF ROUTINE DECISIONS

A number of dangers with regular or apparently ordinary decisions can provide traps for the unwary:

1. **Complacency.** The belief that the decision is the same or very similar to ones that have been made many times before can lead to complacency and casualness.

Decisions are rarely the same: if the choice is the same then the external environment in which the decision must work has probably moved on. The very fact that decisions are made over and over again can actually change the outside environment, so, for example, the tenth time that the decision is made can be very different from the first.

2. **Boredom** is another potential pitfall that can result in a decision being neglected, perhaps becoming urgent and causing problems later. Boredom also results in a lack of attention and effort, adversely affecting either the choice of decision or its implementation, or both. Potential solutions include:

    ● Focusing on the longer benefits of the decision rather than any immediate results

    ● Enjoying a specific aspect of the decision (while also taking care to complete the whole process)

    ● Fundamental action. Neither of the previous solutions are entirely satisfactory, so if boredom persists the solution might be to substantially revise the way that those decisions are made or even to change jobs

3. **Delegation** is a popular approach when handling routine decisions. What may be routine to one person can be challenging, stimulating, and developmental to others (possibly

subordinates with less experience). The advantage of delegation is that it enables the task to be approached as if for the first time, and potential improvements made with the introduction of a fresh perspective. Furthermore, completion of the task can benefit from renewed interest and vigor.

 Decisions can often be perceived as being routine when in fact there are critical differences that may be subtle, or hidden and consequently ignored. This is different from complacency as it highlights the fact that mistakes can be made at any time.

AVOIDING THE PITFALLS

When making decisions—and particularly those that may seem routine—it can be helpful to consider the following points:

- Are there any long-term implications of this decision?

- What is the risk if it goes wrong? What is the worst that can happen?

- What action can be taken to minimize this risk?

- Where are the critical points in this decision? (For example, it might be gaining acceptance or implementing the decision.)

LONG-TERM DECISIONS

These are the ones that often seem to have the most at stake and the highest profile, but crucially this is not always the case. An essential aspect of leadership is the ability to develop a vision, set direction, and then steer a steady course toward the desired outcome. However, recent research has highlighted a number of critical factors surrounding long-term decisions.

- **Many decisions have long-term consequences and these are often impossible to predict.** An example of this is the process of recruiting new members of staff. In certain organizations this can become a routine activity, yet because it is routine does not mean that it is not also of major, long-term importance

- **All decisions are subject to unforeseen external influences, but long-term decisions are most susceptible to change** because of the length of time over which they can be affected. It is important to monitor long-term decisions regularly and make adjustments when needed, and this clearly requires commitment to be sustained over any length of time

- **Understanding the time scale for decisions is also important.** How long are they likely to last and when will new choices be needed? It is important to be realistic—do not expect decisions to last indefinitely, and do not get caught by surprise!

The decisions commercial managers make about prices are an example of a long-term decision. A price is set and it clearly has to last, but as important as setting the price is knowing *when* to change it and *in what way*. This emphasizes the point that as well as considering external forces—what they are and how they will influence the decision over the long term—it is also worth considering trends and how these forces might develop.

Bill Gates made possibly one of the greatest ever long-term business decisions during the early days of the computer industry. At the time IBM, by far the largest and most influential computer company, needed an operating system and approached Bill Gates (and his partner, Paul Allen). They adapted their QDOS system, called it DOS, and, crucially, *licensed* the rights to IBM. IBM believed that the commercial future lay in the computer hardware that they manufactured, and were unconcerned at not owning the rights to the operating system. IBM did not even acquire the rights to DOS on an exclusive basis. Gates, however, believed that the future lay in software and as long as IBM, the largest computer manufacturer, adopted his system and set the industry standard then he would be able to license the operating system to other manufacturers. His company would also be able to sell software applications (such as word processing, database, spreadsheets, etc.) that integrated with the operating system. This long-term decision was proved correct: Gates and Allen's company, Microsoft, controlled the operating system that came to dominate the industry, and their software generated billions of dollars in revenue and personal fortune. IBM, by contrast, were incorrect: the prospects for computer hardware were not as good as for the software business, and they came under attack from cheaper manufacturers that were also using Microsoft software.

SIMPLE BUT VITAL DECISIONS

Simple decisions can be deceptive. It is easy to rush into a decision believing it to be easy and straightforward only to find a mass of complexity, sub-plots, and sensitivities. If these are present then they should become apparent during the decision-making processes of researching, analyzing, and understanding the relevant information.

It can also help to develop a standard checklist for approaching seemingly simple decisions, including:

- Is this the best option or is there a better way?

- Is there sufficient time to consider and implement this decision effectively, or do we need longer?

- Who is affected by this decision?

- What is affected by this decision? What are the likely consequences?

- It may seem a simple choice, but how practical and risk free is it to implement?

- Where are the milestones, potential pitfalls, and critical points with this decision?

- How will we know when we have achieved success?

- Are additional resources needed?

- What makes the decision vital—what is riding on it?

- Are all of the people involved in the decision fully aware of its importance?

- Is everyone fully motivated to achieve success?

- Where are the likely pitfalls and what are the likely complications or problems?

COMPLEX DECISIONS

FACTS TO APPRECIATE ABOUT COMPLEX DECISIONS

Complex decisions often require large amounts of work and tend to be big decisions, with the result that pressure can develop into stress at certain times or for people in critical positions. This needs to be understood and monitored, and support provided when necessary.

Complex decisions are often delayed or rushed because it can be so arduous to complete them properly. The key is to adopt the right attitude, and to understand that reaching the right outcome may be a laborious process but that it is essential. It is also important to manage the external environment, in particular ensuring that enough time is allocated to completing complex decisions. There are several relevant questions to consider including:

- Has this decision been made before—if so, was it successful and why? Alternatively, if it failed previously what were the reasons?

- If the decision has not been made before, are there any similarities with previous decisions?

- Is there anyone whose experience could be sought?

- Can the complexity be reduced (or made more manageable) by breaking the decision into smaller, constituent parts?

- Is a team approach the best method of tackling this issue? If so, is the team fully competent and prepared?

The last two questions point to the key to resolving complex issues: try to simplify them and break them down into their constituent parts. These can each be managed much more effectively, but this process does require strong and effective central monitoring and control to ensure success.

THE CONSEQUENCES OF DECISIONS: THE DECISION WEB

Most decisions have a wide range of consequences, many of which are trivial and unforeseen, but some consequences can be very significant. Furthermore, decisions can also combine and interrelate to form a complex *decision web*. It is useful, therefore, when making a decision to consider the implications and effects (short-, medium-, and long-term) that the choice—and its implementation— will have. (Any fan of the classic 1940s film *It's a Wonderful Life*, directed by Frank Capra and starring James Stewart, will understand the long-term consequences of decisions.)

When assessing and understanding the consequences of decisions, there are several key points to consider.

SELF-FULFILLING PROPHECY
This is when the decision brings about the set of circumstances on which it is based.

For example, a storekeeper may be convinced that there will be a decline in trade because a major supermarket chain is opening a store nearby. Therefore, in an effort to compensate for what is *perceived* as an inevitable reduction in the level of business and profit, the storekeeper raises all of the shop's prices. The result is a decline in business.

As this example shows, self-fulfilling prophecies usually have a key factor driving them (in this case, perceptions arising from the opening of the new store), and these perceptions often cloud the issue, making the decision even harder. For example, in the storekeeper's case any action may have resulted in the same outcome—a decline in business.

To avoid decisions becoming self-fulfilling prophecies you should:

- Check the facts, rather than relying on hearsay or guesswork

- Avoid making assumptions; if estimates are unavoidable then they should be based on as much research as possible

- Take your time—use all of the time available to you as it may allow the situation to become clearer, or other options to emerge

SELF-REINFORCING PROCESSES

Decisions can often act in a positive way to reinforce processes. For example, a business may have a target of attracting 10,000 new customers in a year and the technique to be used is lower prices. This not only attracts new customers in the short term but also builds the reputation of the brand as word spreads, potentially gaining customers in the long term. Self-reinforcing or runaway growth could result.

However, self-reinforcing processes can also have a negative aspect. For example, if a business starts delivering products late—or if they start falling apart—then the firm will gain a negative reputation, and this will be reinforced by word of mouth unless action is taken to reverse it.

In many situations, decisions set precedents for the future. This happens both in a formal sense (the clearest example being a legal decision) and informally, as people tend to look for and expect consistency, and often predict future actions based on past ones.

Having assessed the different types of decision that are typically required, the next chapter focuses on the challenge of increasing confidence, audacity, and enjoyment when making decisions.

step 7

INCREASING CONFIDENCE
AND BOLDNESS

"One of the primary, fundamental faults with American management is that over the years it has lost its zest for adventure, for taking a risk, for doing something that no one has done before."

HAROLD GENEEN

OVERCOMING THE FEAR OF RISK

The conventional, controlling business approach to managing risk predominates. However, rather like viewing the glass as half-empty rather than half-full, it is only one perception, and a fairly limited one.

Clearly, business risks need to be understood and cautiously managed; some people work best in a high-risk environment and certain situations may demand it. Understanding how organizations manage risk effectively is valuable, but *managing* risk is only one possible strategy. Another approach is to look for ways to turn risk into an advantage: using the risk to achieve success, either by adding value or by outstripping competitors, or both.

Unfortunately, organizations take the fun out of risk. It is seen as a necessary evil and managing risk is seen as bureaucratic and stifling—which frequently it is. Organizations fail to see that risk is both *desirable*, providing new opportunities to learn, develop, and move forward, and *necessary*, compelling people to improve and meet the current of challenge and change effectively.

There are several practical techniques for overcoming the fear of risk and for increasing confidence and boldness.

CREATE A POSITIVE CLIMATE

Simply recognizing the need for audacity is inadequate. The ethos of the entire organization must embrace a culture that emphasizes and rewards any behavior that actively manages risk. This requires a commitment by senior managers and the resources (which includes training) to achieve it.

If we are to be audacious ourselves and expect others to follow then we can use several techniques, proactively and determinedly, to ensure success. These are not intended as a linear process, but rather as techniques and areas of focus that are important at specific moments when we are pushing back the boundaries of risk and audacity. These techniques are:

- Establishing a compelling vision

- Handling conflict and emotions

- Communicating, influencing, and negotiating

- Dealing with stress

- Coaching and teamworking

- Decision making and problem solving

DEVELOP AUDACIOUS THINKING

Becoming successfully audacious requires three elements: awareness, self-confidence, and a compelling vision.

1. **Increasing awareness.** Successfully audacious people have high levels of awareness—in particular, self-awareness—that enable them to reflect and question what is going on. This allows them to recognize their own role in terms of their abilities and their impact on others. They are also aware of other people, objectively evaluating their strengths and weaknesses and judging what their likely responses and actions will be.

2. **Building self-confidence and taking control.** There is a dangerous edge to many situations, activities, and opportunities; a point at which we perceive that trauma may occur. To approach this point we need a protective frame, a way of viewing the situation so that we can deal with it. If such

a frame exists, we can view the risk with excitement; without it, we are filled with anxiety. Three levels of control are needed to be audacious: control of the situation, control of contribution, and control of reaction.

3. **Establishing a compelling vision and motivational connection.** A vision does not mean simply a goal, if a goal is only a destination to be measured and dispassionately achieved. A vision also describes the journey to be taken. It is motivationally rich, meaning that it appeals to a broad range of values in those who take part.

STEP INTO THE DANGER ZONE

When taking risks, we need to feel the presence of danger but not to focus on it. This heightens our senses and ensures that the three critical components of an audacious mindset—awareness, self-confidence, and motivational connection—come into play.

Stepping into the danger zone requires us to have a protective "confidence frame" that is built on firmer foundations than simply knowing the odds. Audacious individuals build their confidence frames from three overriding emotions:

1. A sense of self-mastery.

2. A feeling of rebelliousness—willfully defying convention.

3. These two feelings then lead to a third: a sense of control.

Most people distinguish between two sorts of control: controlling the situation and controlling one's reaction. Audacious people seem to be able to add a third element to their control strategy: they know how to control the way they contribute to a situation.

Stepping into the danger zone also requires each individual to develop and heighten their personal awareness. This works when the danger is not simply in our minds but is real and tangible. One of the great insights into sporting performance in recent years has been the understanding of the role of awareness in high performance. Elite athletes seem to have a heightened sense of awareness, not only of what is going on around them, but also of their own internal world. Moreover, they seem to be able to change this focus to deal with an unfolding situation.

Successful, adventurous performance depends on:

- **A high degree of self-knowledge.** How am I doing? What assumptions am I making? How am I emotionally and motivationally responding to the world?

- **An external focus,** sensing what is going on in the environment and what its impact might be

What is crucial is how self-knowledge of our changing and dynamic internal world leads us to interpret the broad and narrow features of our external world. Almost any sort of bold decision or solution will require this ability to change focus.

HANDLE CHANGING AND CONTRADICTORY EMOTIONS

Key points to note include:

- Boldness relies on awareness, and this in turn depends upon our emotional versatility—our ability to be in the right frame of mind at the right time, and . . .

- If we are in a team, others need this ability as well

- Individual awareness matters if we are to seize opportunities by challenging our assumptions about the true nature of the risk. Although some people are more naturally self-aware than others, this is also a skill that can be developed

The greatest problem in building confidence and boldness is usually one of overcoming fear or inertia, and this requires awareness, control, confidence, and a compelling vision or motivation to act.

DEALING WITH STRESS CAUSED BY DECISIONS AND PROBLEMS

A certain amount of pressure is often helpful in maintaining focus. It is important that this does not develop into stress as this is disruptive, distracting, and impairs judgment. This may be difficult to achieve, especially as urgent decisions can sometimes flow in a steady, unremitting stream, notably during a crisis.

THE PERSONAL NATURE OF STRESS

Every individual has their own tolerance limits for stress, but it is important to recognize the symptoms and take action when needed.

The physical symptoms of stress include:

- irregular breathing
- tension and stiffness
- stomach complaints
- exhaustion
- tension headaches
- twitching
- fidgeting and feeling restless or "on edge"
- a dry mouth and throat
- feeling hot
- clammy hands and perspiration
- sexual problems

These problems can all occur at different times and for many reasons quite unrelated to stress; however, they may well be stress-related if several occur at the same time, if they appear constantly, or if they appear with no apparent cause.

The behavioral symptoms of stress are no less significant or serious, and include feeling worried, demotivated, irritated, withdrawn, upset, exhausted or weary, angry, misunderstood, frustrated, and powerless. These in turn lead to impaired judgment and the stressed individual not working normally. It is often difficult to know when one is suffering from stress—or the danger of it—because it invariably builds up over time and is difficult to separate from normal behavior.

Individual reactions to stress vary, and it is also worth pointing out that different people seem to have different levels at which they suffer from stress, based on their own personality and life experiences. In assessing your own level of stress you should understand your personal threshold for stress. If you are unsure, the best approach is to ask yourself if this situation would normally upset you. If you suspect you might be stressed, or especially if someone else mentions it to you, it may be worth questioning your own pattern of behavior—do you behave as you would normally act (or react)?

PREVENTING AND HANDLING STRESS

The following techniques can be valuable for preventing and dealing with stress when making decisions or resolving problems.

- **Know yourself.** Understand what causes *you* stress, when you are likely to become stressed, and how you can avoid these situations

- **Take responsibility.** Too often people either deny their problem, in which case it will almost certainly worsen, or blame someone (or something) else. Even if it is the fault of someone else, it is *you* that is affected and *you* who needs to resolve it

- **Consider what is causing stress.** Knowing the symptoms and acknowledging the existence of stress is really only the start: the next step is to identify the source of the stress. This is complicated by the fact that stress is often caused by an accumulation of factors. The solution is to consider rationally how to take down the wall that is encircling you, brick by brick. Stress is rarely removed in one swift leap, but often requires action in a range of areas

- **Anticipate stressful periods (either at work or at home) and plan for them.** This may include getting temporary resources or people with specific skills to help during a particular period

- **Develop strategies for handling stress.** Consider what may have worked for you in the past, what you did, and how successful it was

- **Understand and use management techniques to prevent or reduce stress.** For example, many difficulties are caused either by time pressures or by relationship issues that could be prevented by more assertive or controlled behavior, so brush up on your time management and assertiveness skills

- **Relax.** Easier said than done, but the key is to understand that you need to *work* at relaxing

step **8**

BEING CREATIVE AND INNOVATING

"Creativity is thinking new things. Innovation is doing new things."

THEODORE LEVITT

"You can innovate by not doing anything, if it's a conscious decision."

HERB KELLEHER

CREATIVITY: THE ART OF THE DECISION

What counts is not what we know, but how we react to what we do not know.

In business, as in life, experience is valuable only as long as the future resembles the past. This is true at one level: experience is a useful ally, but it should not dominate. Experience enables us to understand and cope with change. However, in business, the art of decision making has two facets: how we react to what we do *not* know, as well as how we react to clearly defined situations. And when faced with the unknown, there is little choice but to create: to innovate and discover.

Decision making requires something more than just applying tried and tested formulae to your predicament, more than using the past—it requires an originality and flair of mind that determines one's creative intelligence.

Innovation and creativity matter for several reasons.

- They provide highly effective techniques for coping with the unknown. This enables you to ride the inexorable waves of change to drive your organization forward

- Harnessing and focusing experience improves creative abilities. It is experience that points the way to likely futures—situations or "rules" that are fast approaching. And any insights you produce will be formed as a product of your experiences

However, it is important to be clear about how experience relates to creativity. Experiences highlight the areas for insight, help give a "common sense" idea of what works, and show the importance of being original. They should not act as a constraint; just because something didn't work or didn't happen does not mean it never will.

- Being creative and innovating is one of the few ways of proving that we are unique, scarce, and valuable. This matters as people are under increasing pressure to set themselves apart and compete by being original

- Decision making and problem solving are more of an art—experience plays a part, but creative insight is fundamental. However, unlike other arts, creative problem solving and decision making rely on the successful adoption of certain techniques

- Innovation and insight can be actively managed and produced, as long as the psychological and systematic rules are understood and acted on

GENERATING SOLUTIONS

In many organizations, too much attention is paid to norms, rules, procedures, and precedents, to the detriment of creative thinking. However, many of the problems that organizations face today cannot be solved without a creative approach—some of the most popular and effective approaches are described below.

PARETO ANALYSIS

Frequently recurring problems may, in fact, be several completely different problems, all linked to each other and with many causes. In such circumstances, *Pareto analysis* can be useful in organizing the data so that the most significant factors are clearly illustrated. This method is based upon the 80–20 Pareto principle: that 80% of problems are caused by 20% of the possible factors. Tackling a problem requires a focus on the troublesome 20%.

The four steps in Pareto analysis are:

1. Identifying the overarching problem.

2. Determining the causal factors and how often they occur.

3. Listing the biggest factors. Pareto analysis applies when few factors are involved.

4.   Developing a solution targeting each factor individually.

This approach can eliminate the main causes of a problem, and often prevent it recurring or, at least, mitigate its effects. It is less useful when a large number of factors are more or less equally responsible, as it is difficult and time consuming to treat each one and pointless to prioritize the order that they are dealt with. Pareto analysis works best when damage control is the only possible action. For example, all organizations get customer complaints, but the main reasons for customer dissatisfaction can be attended to, thus reducing the incidence of complaints. However, the more complicated the problem, the less likely it is that Pareto analysis will help to find a solution. For complex problems, creative or intuitive problem solving is required.

EXPERIENCED PROBLEM SOLVING: HEURISTICS

An *heuristic* system is one that uses experience to guide future plans and decisions.

- It is characterized by flexibility and tentativeness rather than force or certainty

- Decisions are adapted and adjusted as events develop, all the while guided by a specific set of values. Because of this, heuristic methods work best in situations where structured or systematic decision-making methods cannot be applied, perhaps because the situation is completely new

- Heuristics are completely relevant to the world of business. Core principles (such as meeting customer needs or acting as an effective leader) combined with experience can be applied quickly and flexibly to effect a solution

- The opposite of detailed scenario planning or computer modeling, heuristic approaches are probably the most popular and successful way of providing an adaptable problem-solving mechanism

KEPNER-TREGOE ANALYSIS

It is a mistake to assume that every solution to a problem requires innovation and creativity. Often, all that is needed is the ability to find out why something that should work is failing and to fix it. This approach is at the heart of *Kepner-Tregoe analysis*. Its emphasis on solid, rational analysis makes it suited to "hard" rather than "soft" management issues. For example, it is used to explain deviations from the norm, quality or process problems (often in manufacturing), how to repair machines or systems, and to identify potential problems.

Applying Kepner-Tregoe analysis is remarkably simple, methodical, and powerful. The first stage is to define the problem in detail by answering several key questions precisely:

- *What* is the problem or deviation?

- *Where* does it occur?

- *When* does it (or did it) occur?

- *How* does it occur? Specifically, how often does it happen, and *how old* is the process when it first occurs?

- *How big* is the problem (how much is affected in real terms or as a proportion of the whole)?

By observing the situation and answering these questions it is possible to clearly define what the problem is—as well as what the problem *is not*. Using this information, the next stage is to examine the differences between what should happen and what does happen— preparing a list of possible causes either for each problem in turn, or, if they are linked in a process, for the problem as a whole.

MIND MAPPING

This is an approach that organizes thoughts and ideas into a clear form, from which patterns and new approaches emerge or crystallize. *Mind maps* help to clarify issues, as well as sharing and communicating ideas. A starting point is to list the pros and cons of each idea. Grouping issues into specific categories can also be useful; a popular example of this is SWOT analysis, which identifies internal strengths and weaknesses, and external opportunities and threats. Finally, displaying ideas in diagrammatic form can highlight relationships between ideas.

GENERATING HIGHLY INNOVATIVE SOLUTIONS

Problem solvers are often constrained by the traditional boundaries of their own narrow range of experiences and the narrow expectations placed upon them. Becoming better at problem solving is often about thinking of better solutions faster, rather than being purely about implementation. The prevailing trend for people to think in terms of functional boxes must be reversed if problem solving is to improve. Innovation is about thinking *outside of these boxes*, forgetting the boundaries, and achieving breakthrough solutions and ideas.

To foster innovation, undertake the following activities.

USING VERTICAL AND LATERAL THINKING

Creativity can be divided into *left brain activities*, which are logical and analytical, and *right brain activities*, which are creative and integrative. A systematic approach to creativity is provided by the author of 62 books to date on creative thinking and inventor of the term *lateral thinking*, Edward de Bono, who distinguishes between:

- **Vertical thinking,** which is bounded by logic and linear thinking, and

- **Lateral thinking,** which cuts across normal boundaries and processes

De Bono's view is that many techniques are inadequate for solving certain problems; in these situations lateral thinking is useful for generating new ideas and approaches.

Lateral thinking is an approach that combines ideas and concepts that have not previously been brought together. Another aspect of lateral thinking is to remove binding assumptions by asking *what if?* questions. Understanding how you think, though, is only the beginning of improving the thought processes.

ADOPTING A QUESTIONING APPROACH

Questioning is a useful starting place for creativity: challenging is the way that alternatives are generated. This must happen in a supportive environment and is the essential first step in breaking traditional thinking. It often helps to question established logic, asking *why?* alongside *why not?* Questioning the limits of existing processes and systems may stimulate real "solutions."

ACCEPTING THAT GOOD IDEAS CAN COME FROM ANYWHERE

Many people still assume that those who are paid the most money are the most likely to have the best ideas. In truth, ideas are no respecters of status or salary! While it may be true that in certain industries seniority is an important factor in determining insight, actually, anyone is capable of a winning idea. It cannot be damaging to look at the valuable contributions of junior members of staff, competitors, or even historical legend: successful leaders must be open to all approaches.

DRIVING REALISTIC INNOVATION

- Embracing radical change, even re-engineering, is useful. Experience is valuable but it isn't everything

- By removing barriers to innovation, full use may be made of resources

- Motivating people and empowering them is an important way to continue driving innovation, and this means rewarding innovators wherever possible. This helps to ensure that the process continues successfully and that new ideas and approaches to problem solving gather momentum

- Where feasible, innovative ideas need to be tested, planned, and related to the practical realities of a situation

- It is important to select the right person to check whether a solution is feasible—ensuring they do not make any decisions based on vested interests

- Recognizing early if the innovations are far-fetched or impractical allows the approach to be altered accordingly

PLANNING THE IMPLEMENTATION OF NEW IDEAS

Good ideas may still fail because of poor planning or execution. The skills needed to generate breakthrough thinking—such as breaking the rules—are different from the skills needed for successful implementation—such as having a good understanding and practice of the tried and tested rules of the game. Even successfully implemented ideas can fall apart if they are not monitored, refined, and embedded in the organization. Patient, critical analysis is again much more important here than it is for the initial process of innovation.

RELEASING CREATIVITY

Understanding the factors preventing creativity is vital in eliminating them. As well as factors specific to each organization and individual, other general issues can reduce or frustrate creativity. These include lack of confidence, usually resulting from a fear of failure or concern about how creativity will be viewed by others. Perfectionism and self-criticism are often closely allied to a lack of confidence or feelings of insecurity. It can be useful to encourage training, personal development, and mentoring, backed up by positive support.

Where possible, putting the person in a position where their talents can flourish and achieve greatest benefit can also help to improve effectiveness. Organizational cultures that include negativity or blame, or hierarchies that are too formal and rigid, can often frustrate creativity. People can be resistant to the change that creativity implies; again, this may result from a fear of failure, or a fear of uncertainty and ambiguity. Clear direction and support from the leader and the team can help to allay these fears. Finally, innovations and ideas can be lost due to a lack of courage, conviction, or decisiveness—or by analyzing the idea to its death.

BRAINSTORMING AND MORPHOLOGICAL ANALYSIS

Brainstorming encourages people to release all their ideas on a specific topic, usually led by a facilitator, in an atmosphere of constructive suggestion rather than criticism, discussion, or even comment. The ideas are then discussed, explored, and prioritized— usually creating new solutions using elements from several suggestions.

Morphological analysis takes the brainstorming approach further, by combining and blending different elements (such as a solution from one suggestion, a method of application from another, with the system of checking progress of yet another) to derive new ideas. Once generated, each idea is then critically evaluated and tested before a decision is reached. The barrier to this useful technique may be a lack of confidence or creative insight—or a lack of willingness to compromise.

With both approaches, the keys to success are to ensure that the ground rules are clearly understood by everyone and are fairly applied.

FINDING THE RIGHT SOLUTION

Once you understand what the problem is and have opened your mind to all the possibilities, you can begin developing a solution to the problem.

- Start by asking whether the problem relates to a permanent, underlying, or structural issue, or whether it is the result of an isolated event

- Some decisions are generic, so are best addressed consistently, whereas isolated events are exceptional and are best resolved when they arise

- Also, the response depends on the specific details of each situation. What may appear to be an isolated event may be an early indicator of a generic problem

- When an organization faces something that is new but that has been experienced by others, the response requires a blend of standard, "best practice" techniques and an appraisal of what is distinctive about the circumstances faced

CHECKLIST: ENSURING THE SUCCESS OF CREATIVE DECISIONS AND SOLUTIONS

1. QUESTION AND CHALLENGE

Question established logic by asking *why?* as well as *why not?* questions. Challenge the limits of existing processes, systems, or technology in a positive way to stimulate creativity. Identifying false assumptions is another valuable step.

2. SEEK OUT GOOD IDEAS

Excellent ideas can come from anywhere—so don't be afraid to go to unusual places or situations to find them.

3. ENSURE INNOVATIONS ARE REALISTIC

Whenever feasible, innovative solutions should be tested against practical realities. Those who generate ideas are not necessarily the best ones to check the practical implications—though, in some cases, they may be the only ones who can.

4. PLAN THE IMPLEMENTATION OF NEW IDEAS

New ideas often fail because of poor planning or execution. They can also fail because of a lack of communication and cooperation between the innovator and the implementer in making sure the vision is fulfilled but adapted as necessary. Patient, critical analysis is more important in planning the implementation of new ideas than it is for the initial process of innovation.

5. ENCOURAGE THE PRINCIPLES OF BRAINSTORMING

As noted above, brainstorming is a process in which a group employs all of its creative talent to come up with many solutions to a problem. However, it is only through the adoption of several important principles that it is likely to work.

- **Quantity matters.** Generate as many ideas as possible. Quality is secondary to the quantity of ideas. The quality of each idea can be assessed later

- **Suspend judgment.** Prevent criticism or evaluation until as many ideas as possible have been produced, so that participants feel free to contribute without fear that their ideas will be torpedoed by others

- **Freewheel.** Encourage every idea, even those that may seem wild and silly. The ideas that at first seem outlandish can be the ones of greatest brilliance

- **Cross-fertilize.** Allow participants to build upon each others' ideas in order to spawn new solutions that represent their collective thinking. This is how brainstorming becomes truly productive

- **Don't rush to judgment.** Allow time between the generation of ideas and the evaluation process. Use a methodical process of elimination to select the optimal solution. Set the criteria on which to rate the ideas generated. This helps to whittle down the ideas to a few promising solutions, of which one should be labeled frontrunner and the others kept as alternatives

DEVELOPING SOLUTIONS QUICKLY: THE DEEP DIVE

 A deep dive process is a focused, team approach to developing solutions to specific problems or challenges. It is intended to harness the ideas of everyone in a team in a creative, stimulating, focused, energetic, fun, and useful way.

A *deep dive* is a combination of brainstorming and prototyping. A deep dive can be completed in an hour, a day, or a week. The main stages in the deep dive process are:

1. Building team variety.

2. Defining the design challenge.

3. Visiting experts.

4. Sharing ideas.

5. Brainstorming and voting.

6. Developing a fast prototype.

7. Testing and refining the prototype.

8. Focusing on the prototype and producing a final solution.

Other valuable aspects of creative problem solving that may be applied when time is a major concern include:

- Trying first (and asking for forgiveness later)

- Test marketing

- Ensuring that teams are as varied and diverse as possible

- Seeking external input

- Reducing—and virtually eliminating—hierarchy

- Generating a sense of play, and working without boundaries

- Being flexible about working arrangements

- Accepting that it is all right to try and fail

- Imposing a deadline while allowing people time to be creative

Solutions need to be practical and achievable within the organization's resources, otherwise they are merely a fantasy, a mirage, and not a solution at all. The true test of any creative or innovative solution is the ability to make it work in practice.

step **9**

IMPLEMENTING DECISIONS

"Effective decision makers always test for signs that something atypical or unusual is happening, always asking: Does the definition explain the observed events, and does it explain all of them? They always write out what the definition is expected to make happen . . . and then test regularly to see if this really happens. Finally, they go back and think the problem through again whenever they see something atypical, when they find unexplained phenomena, or when the course of events deviates, even in details, from expectations."

PETER DRUCKER

GAINING SUPPORT

One frequently overlooked aspect of decision making is the need to gain support, not only to ensure that the decision is the right one but also to facilitate its implementation. Without adequate support, decisions can often be undermined, ineffective, and ultimately flawed.

Implementing decisions is the central element of the entire process. Even the best decisions can be undermined by poor implementation. Carefully thought out, thorough measures are necessary for successful implementation. This part of the process is fraught with pressure, distractions, and the need to control issues at the required level of detail, while also maintaining an overall view of progress.

THE NEED FOR SUPPORT

People do not want to be bothered with incessant requests for their opinions and support, and it is important to show decisiveness and an ability to act quickly and confidently. However, by gaining support for *key decisions*, mistakes can be prevented and the process as a whole can be improved.

Involving other people ensures that:

- Objectives are quickly agreed

- Information is more clearly understood

- New ideas and options are suggested, whether for the decision itself or the most effective method of implementing it

- People are aware of what is happening and do not inadvertently interfere or cause problems

A lack of support for decisions usually results in disaster. In contrast, decisions that enjoy widespread support can achieve even greater success than originally anticipated.

KNOW WHEN TO GAIN SUPPORT FOR KEY DECISIONS

- It is usually best to get support when the decision has significant consequences for people, money, or business processes. These consequences may be far-reaching or they may simply be a departure from the norm

- Recognize that if the decision directly affects other people (or other decisions) then their support will be required, especially if the decision is likely to need additional resources

- If it looks likely to test the limits of authority then support may also be needed

The following techniques are useful for gaining support.

COMMUNICATE

Present and explain the decision clearly to avoid misunderstandings. This also sells the decision actively by highlighting the benefits and value of the approach and warning where the pitfalls and problems may lie. Communication needs to take place throughout the decision-making process so that support is sustained and people do not lose touch or interest in developments. Regular, routine communication can be invaluable should problems arise.

LISTEN TO SUGGESTIONS WITH AN OPEN MIND

People will almost certainly provide their support if they feel that they have had some measure of input into the decision, or feel ownership of some part of the decision-making process. It therefore helps to listen to ideas and comments with an open mind, taking them on board wherever possible. This approach also shows a commitment to considering every avenue in the quest to make the decision work, and that, too, will engender respect and support. Finally (and perhaps most importantly), suggestions may well make a better decision, making it easier to achieve and even reducing the need for support.

SHOW TACT AND SENSITIVITY

Closely linked to the previous point is the need to show sensitivity and understanding when making decisions. It is hard to gain support if other people's wishes or aspirations are trampled on, and simply appearing insensitive may result in hostility, concern, a lack of support, and even obstruction.

BE DILIGENT, METHODICAL, AND CONSCIENTIOUS

People are much more likely to embrace an idea that is well thought out. A half-baked notion is unlikely to impress anyone; on the contrary, people may try to stop it happening, fearing the consequences of failure.

SHOW COMMITMENT AND ENTHUSIASM

These virtues usually engender support as, in the main, people respond well to the infectious nature of enthusiasm (provided it is not too overwhelming!). People also like to help, and enthusiasm often provides a clear opening for help and support to be offered.

INCREASING THE LIKELIHOOD OF SUCCESS

As you might expect, there is no sure-fire method of ensuring success. However, there are several basic rules for implementing decisions that will increase effectiveness and the likelihood of success, as well as providing a foundation for correcting things should they go awry.

BE HONEST AND ADOPT AN ETHICAL STANCE

Quite apart from their intrinsic moral value and benefits, honesty and integrity are the most easily defended virtues. People understand that honesty is the best policy and respect people that demonstrate this virtue. Put another way, dishonesty will probably lead to difficult decisions becoming worse, and future decisions may prove impossible as people's trust and respect will hemorrhage should they encounter deceit (even if they do not themselves directly suffer as a result).

However, honesty in decision making does not mean being insensitive; it simply means *doing the right thing*. This calls for tact, sensitivity, and understanding; all of these are preferable to dishonesty and other unethical behaviors, which are counterproductive over time, if not in the short term.

BE PRACTICAL—THE DECISION NEEDS TO BE WORKABLE NOW AND IN THE FUTURE

Decisions can fail because although they seem logical in theory, in practice they are unworkable. Political decisions often provide the most dramatic examples of this, where politicians have reached a perfectly sensible decision, only to find that it cannot work in practice because it is deeply unpopular commanding little or no support.

WATCH FOR SETTING A PRECEDENT

Decisions often set precedents, and this may be useful or it may be a hindrance. Consider whether:

- The decision sets a precedent

- The methods chosen for implementation establish expectations for the future

- There are precedents that provide a useful guide, showing others how to make decisions and solve problems

However, precedents may also establish bad practices as standard. This is further complicated by the fact that approaches used in decision making—the techniques and methods—are often specific to each set of circumstances and cannot simply be mimicked.

BE METHODICAL

Major decisions need to be planned carefully and methodically. Events may, or may not, occur in linear progression.

Careful planning and monitoring of a decision will help to ensure that the right action is taken at the right time, as well as preventing problems from building.

With any decision, a methodical approach will also help to ensure that each stage is fully completed before the next one starts. This is important, as casualness, haste, and lack of focus can result in decisions being poorly implemented and, perhaps, ultimately failing.

USE ALL AVAILABLE RESOURCES

People often focus too much on one aspect of the decision; most obviously this is *what* to do, and devote insufficient time to other issues of *how* and *when* to act. This may be because they favor and prefer one area, or because they are fearful or insecure of other aspects of the decision. This can prove to be a weakness, as *every* aspect of the decision needs adequate consideration. Success relies on:

- Standing back from the process and deciding early what resources will be needed to implement the decision, monitor its effectiveness, and ensure success

- Not making assumptions (for example, assuming that there are no additional resources, or simply being unaware of the resources that are available)

- Finding the right resources including time, information, people, and money

A key attribute of skillful decision makers is their ability to manage resources so that they have enough of each at the right time. In particular, this means finding ways of gaining additional resources, and the easiest method—asking—is often overlooked!

MANAGE RISK

Decision making demands boldness and creativity, even audacity on occasions. However, to increase the likelihood of success this needs to be tempered with an understanding of when and how to minimize risk, being prudent, and approaching with caution.

Several questions can help when managing risk:

- What might be the consequences of failure (worst case)?

- What is the likelihood of failure?

- What are the alternatives? (In particular, what are the consequences and likelihood of them failing?)

- How can the element of risk be minimized?

This approach to risk needs to directly reduce both the likelihood and consequences of failure. For example:

- Additional resources (for example, people or time) might help

- Communicating might gain valuable support

- Planning can ensure that critical points in the process are considered and prepared for

DEVELOP YOUR OWN DECISION-MAKING STYLE

Establishing a consistent, personal approach to decision making is important. It can help to step back from the process and take time to consider how you typically approach decision making:

- Where are the strengths and weaknesses in your approach?

- What action is needed to improve and develop your skills and abilities?

The advantages of this approach are that:

- The quality of decisions will improve but also a greater measure of consistency will result, making it easier for others to understand and emulate your actions

- Developing a clear and consistent approach to decision making provides a vital fallback position: when pressure increases, complexity rises, or urgency escalates, there is a reliable, tried, and tested approach to fall back on that works for you, and that has been honed during less stressful or critical times

Decision-making style links closely with leadership style and it is worth considering how you lead generally, as well as how you make decisions.

TAKE CONTROL AND SHOW COURAGEOUS LEADERSHIP

Decisions are the essence of leadership: the two are inextricably interwoven and it is impossible to have one without the other. Decision making demands an ability to know when to press ahead and when to change course, as well as the ability to show active leadership, purpose, and direction. This is essential in order to focus resources, determine priorities, and generate commitment and action.

STAY POSITIVE AND RESOLVE PROBLEMS EARLY

The final element in successfully implementing decisions is the need to stay positive and constructive, even in the face of adversity, and maintain a "can-do" attitude. This is not to say that problems or situations should be treated lightly, but a positive mental attitude is widely recognized as being an important source of strength and advantage.

Behaviors to avoid in decision making include procrastination and panic. Instead, adopting a calm, positive, and appropriate approach that displays the right qualities (such as urgency, caution, toughness, flexibility) at the right moment will enhance the likelihood of success.

COMMUNICATE DECISIONS

The support of others is vital for determining a particular course of action and then implementing it successfully. If information about the decision is not communicated, then alienation, mistrust, or uninformed action may result in the objective being undermined and failing. Unfortunately, it is not always easy to gain support for a decision, or more often the need for support is simply overlooked.

GETTING THE BEST FROM PEOPLE

It is said, often insincerely or patronizingly, that people are the greatest resource of any organization. However, when it comes to decisions, they really are. People largely determine the success or failure of management action and it is vital to manage people proactively during the decision-making process. In particular, it is essential to provide management action that focuses on the needs of the task, the team, and the individual and that releases people's talents and ideas, motivating and gaining their commitment to a team approach.

COMMUNICATING AND INFLUENCING

When communicating and influencing people there are several useful techniques.

- **Listen.** Active listening is central to effective communication—people respond better when they feel that their views are being sought and heard. Silence can also be a powerful tool, conveying a range of emotions from disapproval to interest, concentration, or concern, depending on the time and manner of its use

- **Build trust and respect.** People are more likely to give their active support if they feel that they have had the opportunity to contribute and voice their own views. Trust and understanding can be built in many ways: empathizing and putting yourself in the other person's position; "speaking the language" of the people you are trying to relate to; or focusing on what they are *really* saying—not what you think they might be saying. This will help you to overcome people's concerns, keeping their commitment and support for the decision

- **Be sensitive and tactful, choosing your words carefully when necessary.** Tact and sensitivity are important skills when influencing people. Remember, disagreeing at the start with what is being said will usually prompt a defensive or negative reaction. Instead, outline your views first and then explain why you disagree

- **Understand yourself and maintain control.** Recognize your own views, even any prejudices, and avoid letting them influence your behavior. It is important when persuading people to stay in control, although fervor and excitement can be infectious!

- **Be critically aware.** This requires a variety of skills:
  — Reacting to ideas, not people
  — Avoiding jumping to conclusions
  — Listening for *how* things are said, not merely *what* is said
  — Focusing on the significance to the discussion of the facts and evidence

 Aspects of effective influencing and communicating include looking out for body language, both yours and theirs; questioning, not only to improve understanding but also to show interest and attention; and summarizing, to check agreement.

THE IMPORTANCE OF TIMING

Timing is an important element in implementing decisions, and affects each stage in the decision-making process. If action is taken too soon or at the wrong moment, it can fail. Several questions may help to develop a sense of timing and guide one's actions:

- How much time is available to make this decision?

- Can the deadline for a decision be extended?

- How time-sensitive is the decision?

149

- What obstacles might delay the decision being implemented, or what factors could affect the timing of the decision?

- When is the optimum time for making this decision? (Considering what factors are most important will help to decide when the decision needs to happen.)

- Is there a time lag between implementing the decision and it taking effect?

DELEGATING THE IMPLEMENTATION OF DECISIONS

As mentioned in Step 3, effective delegation is based on several simple principles, including the concepts that if people are given authority they will take responsibility, and that the people closest to the action are usually best placed to make decisions and implement them successfully.

Delegation means giving someone else the necessary authority to make decisions and act in a specified area of work, and it is important that delegation is completed successfully for decisions to succeed. By giving someone else the authority to act it is necessary to accept that we are at the same time giving them the "right" to be wrong.

The process for effective delegation remains the same at any level. Having first built up trust the leader needs to:

1. Prepare for delegation, and in particular be clear about what to delegate.

2. Match the right person to each task (or each stage of the decision-making process).

3. Communicate clearly and agree objectives.

4. Provide sufficient resources for effective implementation.

5. Monitor progress, reviewing and assessing overall performance.

Know what decisions and tasks to delegate, and what to avoid delegating

Leaders delegate decisions that they don't need to take themselves. They not only increase their own efficiency, but also develop others to take decisions, and ensure that those decisions are taken by the people best placed to act and achieve success, for example, by delegating specialist tasks and decisions to those with the appropriate skills.

In deciding which tasks and decisions to delegate, consider the following questions:

- What must you do yourself?

- What could others do with your help?

- What could others do better than you?

- What must others do?

- Who would you delegate to, and what tasks would you give each person?

Understand the decisions that cannot be delegated

Each individual needs to consider their own job and decide which tasks they must do themselves. A sensible approach is to avoid delegating three general areas:

- Policy making and goal setting—these key leadership decisions are not usually delegated

- Specific people management issues—such as discipline, appraisal, dispute resolution—are best dealt with by managers

- Major external decisions—such as those arising during crisis management or legal action—are best completed by the leader

Other activities that normally only someone with the status of a manager can undertake and where delegation should be avoided include:

- Coaching, counseling, and morale issues

- Appraisals

- Disciplinary proceedings

- Confidential tasks and sensitive situations

- Complex situations and tasks which have been specifically
  assigned

Prepare to delegate

It is important to focus on the results that you wish to achieve and
have clear, precise objectives, so that the delegation works
smoothly. This will require careful consideration and planning,
possibly discussion with other colleagues, and it may also be
necessary to consider priorities. Review both the importance and
urgency of the decision or task that you are delegating.

Match person and task

The next step is to identify *which* decisions other people could make,
and where the boundaries of their responsibility lie. The person who
is being required to do the job must understand it and have the skills
and competency to tackle it, even if it is different or challenging.

Discuss and agree objectives

All aspects of the task, from the purpose through to the fulfillment,
should be discussed. Having allocated tasks it is necessary to agree
targets, objectives, resources, and review times and deadlines. When
delegating for the first time it is also worth checking the person's
understanding and gaining explicit agreement where necessary.

Provide resources and the appropriate level of authority

The person delegating the task needs to provide all the necessary
resources, support, and authority to complete the task. It is
important to define responsibilities clearly and be ready to advise
when appropriate. It is also important to agree how events will be
monitored and controlled.

Monitor progress

Delegated decisions need to be clearly controlled. This does not mean interfering when there is no need, but checking progress at pre-planned and specified times. Control also involves verifying that things are on track. Monitoring and control ensure that the delegated task is completed successfully. One of the keys to effective monitoring is ensuring that the person completing the task remains accountable.

Review and assess performance

It is useful to check achievements against the original objectives to help improve the decision-making skills of the person completing the task.

Delegating decisions successfully depends on many different factors: the type of job, the work environment, the experience of the employee, the timing of the situation, and the degree of understanding between the manager and team member. A key element in delegating successfully, and finding a way through all these different factors, is to develop the right attitude: it is only then that you are likely to generate the right attitude in others.

DEVELOPING A POSITIVE ATTITUDE

Delegating decisions works best when a positive attitude is adopted. The person delegating the decision needs to show confidence, trust, and personal security by letting go. This is notoriously difficult to achieve, and being prepared to take risks and support mistakes is a useful first step. Letting go also requires patience, and it may be helpful to focus on supporting the person undertaking the task. The manager needs to handle the delegation in a positive way so that the person making the decision or completing the task is thoroughly committed, task oriented, and develops confidence for the future.

Several techniques are valuable for developing a positive attitude to delegation:

- **Support people's decisions.** It is important to show support and provide help when it is needed. Coaching, support, and advice are far more effective when delegating than criticism or negativity, both of which undermine confidence

- **Take risks and avoid emphasizing mistakes.** People usually realize when they have made a mistake and it helps to give them the opportunity to correct it

- **Be clear about your expectations and don't undermine people.** This is always important to avoid any misunderstanding about what will be achieved and how it might be accomplished

ENSURING THAT DECISIONS ARE IMPLEMENTED BY THE MOST APPROPRIATE PERSON

Several questions can help to assess whether the right tasks are being delegated to the right person.

- Who would expect to take this decision—does it "belong" to a person or job-holder?

- What does the decision involve? What skills and resources are needed and are there any specific problem areas?

- Who is trained and experienced in this area?

- Who has the interest and ability both to make the decision and to complete the task?

- Who would benefit from the experience of completing the task?

- Who is available?

- Would the task help to develop skills and abilities, and could it be assigned for this reason?

 Decisions generated by individuals are more likely to have a greater measure of commitment than ones imposed from outside. Unleashing different views, perspectives, and ideas is one of the key benefits of delegation.

CREATING THE RIGHT ENVIRONMENT FOR PREVENTING AND SOLVING PROBLEMS: KEY QUESTIONS

Problem solving is invariably complex and involved, with root causes and consequences often lying hidden, posing traps for the unwary. There are several issues to consider:

- **Is there a problem at all, and if so does it actually need a solution?** People and organizations rush into changes because they assume that specific circumstances have occurred or may occur, and while preparation is essential for preventing problems this needs to be tempered with a clear understanding of the situation. Even if a problem arises it can sometimes be quicker, easier, and less costly to ride it out

  An example might be a business, fighting for its life, that decides as a last act of desperation to reduce its prices. If other factors, such as poor service, poor quality, or an outmoded product, have led to the firm's decline then competitors may want to learn lessons from the firm, but almost certainly they do not need to act in response to the price cut alone. Even if competitors' sales volumes start to fall, it may be a mistake to assume that it is because of the price cut: it could just as easily be due to a change in the market—an alteration in customers' preferences, for instance.

- **Does the person solving the problem or making the decision have sufficient authority?** Certain issues, such as major decisions on strategy or personnel, are clearly the responsibility of senior executives. Many issues are cross-functional and this complicates "jurisdiction." Furthermore, many issues are simply too complex to be addressed by one person alone, requiring the support of a group to be carried through

- **To what extent should senior or experienced colleagues be involved?** It is often useful to discuss major issues with senior colleagues who may be able to provide a different perspective or additional experience, even if their authority is not required. Acting without sufficient authority may in very rare cases be unavoidable, but if it does happen then the systems almost certainly need to be changed so that it is not repeated. Otherwise, acting without authority can simply cause more problems than it solves, notably problems relating to confidence and trust

- **How best to plan, test, and implement the solution?** Not only does the implementation need to be planned and tested, but action needs to follow through and deliver exactly as planned; this means monitoring the implementation process and changing methods as necessary, but keeping the final goal clearly in mind

- **How can you identify problem areas early and prepare contingency plans?** This is valuable for avoiding problems as well as resolving them quickly

- **Can you identify in advance those people whose help is essential?** This includes those people whose expertise can be called upon should the need arise. If help is required then the sooner it is requested the better. Certain problems or decisions require change agents—people who can lead the process—as well as influencers who can help to motivate people, gaining their support and commitment. If major change is needed then it is essential that those people affected recognize the problem and the solution

- **How can you prevent an atmosphere of negative criticism or blame?** Too often blame is apportioned in a manner resembling a witch-hunt. This can cause short-term problems of division and recrimination that may obscure the implementation of an effective solution. This approach has longer-term consequences too, as people avoid taking action or focus on protecting themselves and justifying their actions at the expense of a solution

- **How will you ensure that problems are owned?** Clear ownership is necessary to drive a solution forward, with the planning, implementation, and monitoring of the solution being completed by the correct person, with further measures taken as needed

 Include the right people in the decision or solution, but only the right people. Involving people who are not required for a particular task can make the process unwieldy, while excluding people or groups who need to be involved provides an even bigger handicap.

- **Are you ensuring (or how will you ensure) ownership of the solution?** If the solution is accepted and actively supported then this is preferable to the decision being imposed or prescribed from outside. Ownership is likely to result in much greater levels of commitment, motivation, and energy

- **Is there a danger of people undermining the problem-solving process?** This can be done, for example, by manipulating people or ideas, or by raising expectations (perhaps by inviting people to suggest solutions) only to reject them. The key is to focus on the needs of the task and the best approach to resolving the situation

 Any solution will need to rely on the skills and commitment of people.

- **Are problem-solving skills and processes for preventing or handling difficulties being honed in a safe and stable environment?** Prior preparation is preferable to struggling to find the right resources and people in the midst of a problem. Without adequate preparation, the problem-solving process can become fearsomely complex, distracted, and overly experimental. Success may be possible but it will certainly be harder to accomplish

In the next chapter, we highlight the hidden pitfalls in decision making: what can go wrong; how and why; and what can be done to ensure success.

step **10**

AVOIDING THE PITFALLS
AND DEVELOPING AN
ACTION PLAN

"Making mistakes is the key to making progress . . . Mistakes are not just golden opportunities for learning; they are, in an important sense, the only opportunity for learning something new . . . Biological evolution proceeds by a grand, inexorable process of trial and error—and without the errors the trials wouldn't accomplish anything."

DANIEL C. DENNETT

THE HIDDEN PITFALLS IN DECISION MAKING

The way that people think, both as individuals and collectively within organizations, affects the decisions that they make, in ways that are far from obvious and rarely understood. Writing in the *Harvard Business Review*, John Hammond, Ralph Keeney, and Howard Raiffa have provided some of the most intriguing research and insights in this area. (See John S. Hammond, Ralph L. Keeney, and Howard Raiffa, "The Hidden Traps in Decision Making," *Harvard Business Review*, September–October 1998.)

Although bad decisions can often be traced back to the way the decisions were made, the fault sometimes lies not in the decision-making process, but in the mind of the decision maker.

 The work of the human brain can frequently undermine our choices and decisions. Avoiding the following traps requires recognizing that they exist and understanding those most likely to cause you problems.

THE ANCHORING TRAP

This occurs when we give disproportionate weight to the first piece of information that we receive. Our immediate reaction to the initial impact of the first information is so significant that it outweighs everything else, "drowning" our ability to evaluate the situation effectively. As a result, the decision or solution is anchored around this one issue. The antidote is to be sure about what is happening and to wait as long as possible to ensure that you have all the information—and to look for different options.

THE STATUS QUO TRAP

This biases us toward maintaining the current situation—even when better alternatives exist—and might be caused by inertia, or the potential loss of face if the current position was to change.

Organizations often have managerial beliefs and approaches that have developed over time from experience and become institutionalized, guiding strategic thinking and action. It is easy to dismiss corporate legend. People may believe that an idea or business formula developed under previously prevailing conditions is still appropriate. Worse still, there may be vested interests in maintaining the status quo, and people may feel insecure about either admitting that things have changed, or recognizing the need for a new approach. The solution for the individual is to value openness, honesty, and courage. Beyond this, the leaders of the organization also need to build a positive, blame-free culture to ensure that the organization as a whole values questioning, experimentation, and learning. People and ideas undermining this culture need to be challenged.

THE SUNK-COST TRAP

The mistakes of the past are often perpetuated because "We have invested so much in this approach/decision that we cannot abandon it or alter course now." The management accountant's view of this is refreshingly sanguine: if it's spent, it's spent—worry about the present and future, not the past. This trap is particularly significant when it comes to managing risk and investing in new projects or deals, such as acquisitions or capital investments.

This situation is also known as an *escalation of commitment*, a flawed way of coping with—rather than simply making—decisions, and is discussed further later in this chapter. The antidote is to plan effectively and know in advance where the plan can be modified and by how much. Maintaining a clear focus on the desired outcome helps, as does keeping an overview of the situation.

THE CONFIRMING EVIDENCE TRAP

Also known as confirmation bias, this is when we seek information to support an existing preference and discount opposing information. It is also a tendency to seek confirming evidence to justify past decisions. People seeking to support the continuation of the current favored strategy frequently manifest this tendency. This way of thinking may lead managers to fail to evaluate the weaknesses of existing strategies, and to overlook important and successful alternatives.

A classic example of the confirming evidence trap is The Waiter's Dilemma—a thinking flaw that is a self-fulfilling prophecy. Consider the situation of a waiter in a busy restaurant. Unable to give excellent service to everyone, the waiter serves only those people that he believes will give a good tip. This appears to work well: only those that he predicts will tip well, do so. However, the waiter fails to realize that the good tip may be the *result* of his actions— and so might the lack of a tip from the other diners. In fact, the only way the waiter can test his judgment is to give poor service to good tip prospects, and excellent service to poor tip prospects. The point here is that original judgments and decisions (such as those made by the waiter) could be less valid than is assumed, as the adequacy of the judgment has not been tested. The solution is for managers to challenge and test existing assumptions, to identify weaknesses in current thinking, and to research alternative approaches to strategic development.

THE OVERCONFIDENCE TRAP

Closely linked to *confirming evidence*, the *overconfidence trap* is when a decision maker overestimates the accuracy of their forecasts because of an exaggerated belief in their ability to understand situations and to predict the future. This is particularly true among business leaders and decision makers, who are not known for being particularly timid or uncertain in their views! This trap is actually more subtle and insidious than it may seem.

One problem with overconfidence is that the solution may sometimes seem obvious, when in fact a better option lies hidden elsewhere. Another danger of overconfidence is casual implementation of the solution.

Many factors can cause overconfidence: a lack of sensitivity, routine, constant success leading to complacency, a lack of criticism or feedback, a confident pre-disposition, or a tendency to make assumptions. Confidence is clearly vital for success, particularly with difficult decisions where a steadfast, determined approach is needed. However, the solution for avoiding overconfidence is to research, investigate, and understand all the possible options and to act appropriately. This means avoiding quick and hasty action. Knowing which approach fits each situation is important for success—another reason why scenario thinking is particularly valuable.

THE FRAMING TRAP

Incorrectly stating a problem or situation completely undermines the decision-making process. This is often, but not always, unintentional. Clearly, how an issue or situation is seen is important in providing the basis for developing an effective strategy or decision. It is worth noting several points:

- Managers habitually follow established success formulae (sometimes known as managerial recipes), and as a result view emerging issues through a single frame of reference

- People's roles and situation within the organization influence the way problems are framed. For example, if one leader is being judged by the staff turnover in their team, then they are likely to frame a departure in a way that does not undermine their position

- The framing trap often occurs because well-rehearsed and familiar ways of making decisions tend to be dominant and difficult to change

- The framing trap may lead managers to solve the *wrong problem*—decisions may have been reached with little thought and better options may be overlooked

- A failure to define the problem may not only lead to the wrong solution being implemented, but the right solution being implemented incorrectly. The causes of this failure include:
  − Poor or insufficient information

— A lack of analysis
— A feeling that the truth needs to be concealed, possibly out of concern
— A desire to show expertise, or a belief that they have to handle it
— A lack of time to frame the problem correctly

Clearly, organizations can go out of business if their managers fail to change their frame so that it encompasses—and allows valid insight into—changes in the business environment. Defining the problem is the foundation to solving it. This requires time, information systems, and analysis skills. It also needs a supportive atmosphere of honesty and fairness where issues and concerns can be openly discussed.

THE RECENT EVENT TRAP

This trap gives undue weight to a recent, and quite probably dramatic, event or sequence of events. This is very similar to the anchoring trap, except that it can arise at any time—not just at the start—and cause a misjudgment. This is also known as *hindsight bias*.

In a study, the research group tended to recollect that they had predicted the occurrence of an event with a high degree of confidence. If a named event had not occurred, they either claimed that they had not predicted it, or that they had placed a low degree of confidence on the poor prediction. The research has demonstrated that we believe that our judgments, predictions, and choices are well made, but this confidence may be misplaced. Awareness of this trap and the danger that it might pose in the way decisions are made is vital for avoiding it.

THE PRUDENCE TRAP

This is being overcautious when we make estimates about uncertain factors. It appears as a tendency to be very risk averse, and is particularly likely to occur when there is a *decision dilemma*: a situation when the decision maker feels that continuing with the current approach carries risks, and that alternative courses of action also carry risks.

In truth, part of successful problem solving and decision making is a willingness and ability to take calculated risks when required, and to minimize those risks. Natural caution, hesitation, and fear of failure are major factors in avoiding risk, but the leader needs to show the way in controlling risk and managing the situation. An unsupportive work environment can also be a factor. The leadership of the organization should therefore set the parameters, clearly demonstrating how and when to manage risk, as well as building a blame-free environment, where experimentation is allowed, properly managed, and controlled.

 It is a flaw to be overcautious. Realism, perhaps erring on the side of caution (depending on the nature of the decision), is the antidote, together with effective, active leadership.

COPING WITH DECISIONS: TYPICAL BEHAVIORAL FLAWS

Leaders cope with decisions and situations in various ways, and these often work against finding or implementing an effective solution.

PROCRASTINATION

Frequently, and almost instinctively, leaders look to lower the level of stress inherent in decision dilemmas. This spawns a number of typical coping patterns, as leaders "wait and see" and try to avoid the risk of failure—often by avoiding a decision.

There are several points to note about decision avoidance or procrastination:

- It can actually result in greater risk, for example, by maintaining an increasingly flawed, outdated, or irrelevant status quo

- Over-reliance on a previously successful formula has damaged many businesses that were, in their time, successful first-movers

- A belief that an established approach remains valid and valuable—even impervious to current external changes—is flawed

- Procrastination and decision avoidance invariably worsen the situation, creating greater complexity and making an effective solution much harder to achieve. They give unhelpful attitudes time to harden and allow time for demotivation and cynicism to take hold. These complicating pressures can, in their turn, frustrate effective decisions

Clearly, procrastination can be caused by many factors. The key, however, is to recognize it when it occurs. Some of the most obvious causes of procrastination include:

- Lack of motivation

- Lack of understanding about the importance of solving the problem

- Fear about the consequences of solving the problem or dislike for the methods that will need to be used

Several approaches can tackle this, including:

- Leading by example: demonstrating commitment, diligence, and other qualities needed to resolve the situation

- Breaking the cycle of procrastination by setting clear priorities for the strategy, yourself, and others

- Empowering people to act, giving them the necessary authority, and making their responsibilities clear

If a decision on an issue beyond the authority of the empowered team is required, then the added pressure of the team usually forces a swift solution.

ESCALATION OF COMMITMENT

In this coping strategy, when decisions or strategy start to fail, the leader responsible for the decision typically commits further resources in an attempt to recover the situation. This stems from a need to defend previous choices. *Escalation of commitment* is characteristic of the manager's need to be proven right, and is, in effect, the sunk-cost trap mentioned earlier.

BOLSTERING

Bolstering occurs when decision makers defensively avoid the stress of difficult decision dilemmas by uncritically emphasizing one option. This happens most often when there is no "good" option available, only a choice among the "least worst" courses of action. There are several key points to note about bolstering:

- Bolstering is a basic way in which decision makers cope with the threats or opportunities that are often part of crucial decisions

- The problem with bolstering is that it can result in a sense of invulnerability to external events, especially when accompanied by an escalation of commitment to the current strategy

- This, in turn, leads to an inadequate search for information and alternatives that might provide a better choice or a more effective solution (nothing will match the artificially "bolstered" choice)

- Bolstering results in poor contingency planning in the event that the favored option fails

SHIFTING RESPONSIBILITY

Shifting responsibility is often a sign of weak leadership. A decision maker will pass ultimate responsibility for the choice to other individuals or groups, usually because of a decision dilemma. Again, this coping pattern is used to reduce the stress of making decisions.

THE PITFALLS OF DECISION MAKING WHICH INVOLVES GROUPS OF PEOPLE

Potential pitfalls can also result from the culture or environment of the organization. The first two, fragmentation and groupthink, can be thought of as the opposite ends of the same spectrum.

FRAGMENTATION

Fragmentation occurs when people disagree with either their peers or their superiors in the organization and has the following features:

- The expression of emerging dissent is usually disguised or suppressed, although it may appear as "passive aggression"

- Dissenting opinion can often fester in the background, for example, mentioned informally in conversation, rather than clearly raised in formal situations, such as meetings

- Each of the fragmented groupings—and there may be several— often show a confirmation bias. In other words, they evaluate incoming information to support initially held opinions, rather than viewing it more objectively

- Fragmentation is corrosive, hindering effective analysis and decision making

- Fragmentation can worsen when the views of one grouping are dominant

- Fragmentation feeds off itself in a loop, with any move to break it cynically seen as an attempt to gain dominance by one side or faction. It can therefore become locked into the organization and be extremely difficult to reverse

GROUPTHINK

Groupthink is the opposite of fragmentation, and is no less of a hindrance to decision making.

- Groupthink occurs when the group suppresses ideas that are critical or not in direct support of the direction in which the group is moving

- The group appears in agreement, and this may be caused by many factors; for example, past success can breed a belief of an infallible team

- Groupthink may occur because the group is denied information, or because individuals lack the confidence or ability to challenge the dominant views of the group

- People may be concerned about disagreeing, because of either past events, present concerns, or a fear of what the future might hold, and so seek safety in numbers

- Groupthink is exacerbated by the fact that cohesive groups tend to rationalize the invulnerability of their decision or strategy, and this in turn inhibits critical analysis and the expression of dissenting ideas. The effect is an incomplete survey of available options, and a failure to examine the risks of preferred decisions

- Groupthink can occur in organizations where teamwork is either strong *or* weak. As with fragmentation, groupthink is also self-sustaining. Moreover, the longer it lasts, the more entrenched and "normal" it becomes in people's minds and behaviors. After a little time, it is also very difficult to reverse

AN EXAMPLE—AND A SOLUTION—TO THE PROBLEMS OF FRAGMENTATION AND GROUPTHINK

These problems are illustrated by the *Abilene Paradox*, written by Jerry B. Harvey. In the story, a man suggests a family trip to Abilene, a town in Texas that was over 50 miles from the family homestead, on a hot, dry, Sunday afternoon. The man asks each person in the room in turn if they would like to go, and each one says yes. However, only when they are returning from their long, uncomfortable, and unpleasant journey does each member of the family confess that they did not want to go in the first place! The first person that was asked—the man's wife—agreed to the trip because she thought that her husband was keen to go. The son-in-law agreed because he thought his parents-in-law (quite possibly authority figures!) wanted to go, and the others in the family agreed because they did not want to spoil the trip for everyone else—so they all reacted positively. However, even the man who suggested the trip in the first place admits that he only did so because he thought that everyone else would prefer to go out, rather than remaining in the house.

Remarkable though it may seem, this situation often occurs in organizations.

- Decisions are made and choices are validated, even though the people involved have hidden reservations

- Decision making is made complex by human nature, with people either seeking to satisfy and support others, or keen to avoid conflict and the risks that this brings

A further frustration arising from the nature of organizations is the phenomena of *organizational lock-in and feedback loops*, mentioned earlier. These occur when the organization is so fixed on a particular belief or view of the world that all of its actions simply reinforce a flawed perception. This can even go so far as to bring about the expected result—i.e. becoming a self-fulfilling prophecy. Information is collated and analyzed through one specific filter, strengthening a fixed perception. Of course, this perception may be accurate—but nothing is forever. The point about lock-in and self-reinforcing feedback loops is that they are unable to sense, with any accuracy, when circumstances are changing, and more importantly, why they may be altering.

The solution to organizational problems of fragmentation and groupthink is to understand their root causes, to consider how, where, and when they might exist, and then to challenge and confront them. Clearly, both problems stem from a lack of honesty and understanding.

THE BIGGEST PROBLEM OF ALL: FAILING TO RESPOND TO CHANGE

The need to change is often complicated by such fundamental issues as funding, regulation, customer perceptions, and technology. Be that as it may, the need to change in the right way at the right time—and in particular, to develop and compete—is axiomatic for any business leader.

If change is so important, what is it about decision making that prevents organizations from achieving it? Put another way, what is it that anchors businesses in their present or past? There are, of course, almost as many answers to these questions as businesses to ask. However, there are several main themes and reasons for failure:

- **A lack of recognizable strategies** in areas such as functional policy, corporate direction, and environmental monitoring. Part of the reason for Enron's failure, for example, was a reliance on financing arrangements, rather than on developing and selling sources of energy. Financial chicanery may have given the impression (and reality) of profit growth and rising shareholder value, but it was no substitute for a strategy to grow and diversify a major energy business. The truth was brutally exposed for Enron when their financial techniques crumbled

- **Weak execution, combined with poor timing of responses to developments,** such as declining customer demand or increasing competition, also causes decline and failure. A clear example of this is the many major airlines that are now grappling with the increasing popularity of low-cost carriers

- **Poor risk taking and poor risk management** are major problems, leaving many organizations overtaken by events. Firms undertake projects that are too large or assess acquisitions too optimistically; for example, AOL and Time Warner, Daimler and Chrysler—massive corporations that faltered in the execution of their strategies, believing that mergers were substitutes for innovation, risk management, and adding customer value. Allied Irish Bank and Barings Bank are more extreme examples of corporations that simply failed to manage risk

The inability to understand and adapt to change is characterized by a leadership that lacks dynamism and is unaware of the need to compete. This typically underpins organizational inertia, uniting the points above. In addition to underestimating the changing market environment, many organizations fail to see the consequences of increased competition—even when the signals are clear.

OVERCOMING THE PROBLEMS OF DECISION MAKING

It is often easy to see decision-making flaws, particularly in others, but much harder to remedy them. Most antidotes are common sense and easily recognizable to any experienced manager. However, it is still worth pointing out the solutions and for this reason they are outlined below.

Potential pitfall	Possible causes	Potential solution
Failure to define the problem—this may lead to the wrong solution being implemented, or the right solution being implemented the wrong way. Either way, the problem persists and potentially worsens.	• Inadequate or insufficient information • Lack of analysis • People hiding the truth out of concern, a desire to show their own expertise, or a belief that they have to handle it • Lack of time	Defining the problem clearly is the key to solving it. This requires sufficient time, information systems, and adequate analysis skills. It also needs a supportive atmosphere of honesty and fairness where issues and concerns can be openly discussed.
Failure to understand the problem and find a solution—sometimes problems can be so complex or fast-moving that finding a solution is difficult. Sometimes there is no satisfactory solution—only a choice between alternatives that are less or more acceptable.	Many of the same factors that stop the problem being clearly defined also combine to prevent it being understood. Information overload or the consequences of the situation can also make it extremely difficult to distinguish between cause and effect.	Understanding the problem will help to highlight possible solutions, or enable a choice to be made between competing options. Ask several key questions: What is the problem? What is not the problem? What is affected by the problem? Who is affected, who is not affected and what is different about those that are affected?

Potential pitfall	Possible causes	Potential solution
Subjective, irrational analysis—this can lead to a solution that fails to solve the problem, or the wrong solution entirely.	This may result from prejudice; being unduly influenced by the "halo" effect (where individuals feel success simply from association with the project, regardless of the likely effectiveness of any decisions); or from expectations or assumptions about behavior or circumstances. Other causes may include casual complacency, arrogance, laziness, tiredness, or overwork.	Check and verify facts and information, avoiding assumptions wherever possible. Objective, rigorous, and unbiased analysis is the best approach.
Laziness or procrastination—avoiding difficult or unpleasant problems invariably makes them worse, or creates time (and other) pressures as additional issues arise and need to be resolved.	This can be caused by lack of motivation; lack of understanding about the importance of solving the problem; fear about the consequences of solving the problem; or dislike for the methods that will need to be used.	• Lead by example, demonstrating commitment, hard work, and the other qualities needed to resolve the situation • Set clear priorities • Monitor key issues and areas of work • Empower people to act by giving them the necessary authority and making clear their responsibilities

Potential pitfall	Possible causes	Potential solution
Lack of sensitivity—failing to appreciate the sensitivity of a situation can result in problems worsening, other difficulties being spawned, and solutions being undermined.	Lack of time, information, and analysis are among the most common causes. A lack of sensitivity may also be a factor, for example, being insufficiently tuned in to people's thoughts and feelings, or failing to show respect.	People are invariably the key to success or failure in problem solving. Influencing, leading, communicating, trusting, and empowering can all help to develop and display sensitivity.
Lack of focus and direction—at best, this erodes efficiency; at worst, it results in the wrong solution or implementation—or no solution at all.	This can occur when there is an absence of leadership or a crisis of leadership, with the person in charge simply failing to lead well enough.	Establish clear priorities and objectives. People need to know what to do, how to do it, and have the necessary skills and resources to ensure success.
Lack of creativity and innovation—relying on experience or past approaches, even when tried and tested, is no guarantee to future success. Certain problems may require a new approach for them to be resolved.	People may not see the need for creativity, or they may not have the skills or resources to be sufficiently creative.	The adage that "if you always do what you've always done, you'll get what you've always got" is important, highlighting the need for an approach that emphasizes continuous improvement. One way forward is to question everything about the problem, even reconsidering factors that may seem fundamental. Alternatively, don't look for major leaps forward or visionary breakthroughs, but instead adopt an approach that emphasizes slow, incremental improvements.

Potential pitfall	Possible causes	Potential solution
A focus on peripheral issues, rather than substance—sometimes the facts surrounding a problem are distracting or demanding in their own right, with the result that the problem is tinkered with or simply left to grow.	A lack of information or analysis, or the daunting nature of a difficult, sensitive, important, or highly complex situation. People may take shelter in little issues or problems, rather than struggle to solve the whole thing—expending large amounts of energy and risking failure.	Consider first principles: what is happening, why, what are its consequences and how can it be resolved. Maintain a clear focus on the problem-solving process. Discussing the situation with others can develop a sense of perspective.
Overconfidence—sometimes the solution may seem obvious, when in fact a better solution lies hidden elsewhere. Solutions can be casually implemented because of overconfidence. Never assume that the best solution to any problem is easily available.	A lack of sensitivity, routine, constant success leading to complacency, a lack of criticism or feedback, a confident pre-disposition, or a tendency to make assumptions.	Confidence is often vital for success, particularly with difficult decisions where a steadfast, determined approach is needed. However, acting appropriately means avoiding quick and hasty action where possible. Know which approach fits each situation.
Being too risk averse—part of successful problem solving and decision making can be a willingness and ability to take calculated risks. Hesitation and fear of failure are natural, but the leader needs to show the way in controlling risk and managing the situation.	Natural caution is one of the biggest factors in avoiding risk, but an unsupportive work environment can also be a factor.	The leadership of the organization or team needs to set the parameters, clearly demonstrating how and when to manage risk, as well as building a blame-free environment, where experimentation is allowed and properly managed and controlled.

USING SCENARIO THINKING TO OVERCOME PROBLEMS

The *strategic conversation* is the continuous process of planning, analyzing the environment, generating and testing scenarios, developing options, selecting, refining, and implementing. It is a central part of the increasingly popular and successful approach of *scenario planning*. Scenarios are effective because:

- They provide a framework for combining the formal and informal elements of the strategic conversation

- They enable decision makers and strategists to examine a wide range of information, to understand the drivers of the present and the future, and to articulate and challenge their assumptions as to how and why the future may evolve

- The outcome of the scenario process is a deeper understanding of alternative views, and a new and more sophisticated language approach to strategic decisions, largely resulting from an enhanced "strategic conversation"

 Scenarios may not predict the future but they do illuminate the causes of change—helping managers to take greater control when conditions shift.

 If enacted effectively, scenario thinking challenges managers' mental models and orthodoxy in a way that fosters a shared understanding and leads to joint action.

Scenario thinking is such a potent technique for "wind tunneling" decisions and solutions—as well as understanding, preventing, and pre-empting problems—that its benefits deserve explanation.

THE BENEFITS OF SCENARIOS

- **Understanding the present.** Scenario thinking provides a better understanding of how different factors affecting a business affect each other. It can reveal linkages between apparently unrelated factors and, most importantly, it can provide greater insight into the forces shaping the future, delivering real competitive advantage

- **Overcoming complacency.** Scenarios should be designed to challenge established views, overcoming "business-as-usual" thinking and enabling established formulae and new ideas to be tested. Seeing reality from different perspectives mitigates the pitfalls of groupthink, procrastination, hindsight bias, bolstering commitment to failing strategies, and shifting responsibility

- **Promoting action and ownership of the strategy process.** Scenario thinking helps break the constraints on traditional strategic practices as it enables those involved to discuss the complexity and ambiguity of their perspectives in a wide context

- **Stimulating creativity and innovation.** Scenarios encourage the opening of minds to new possibilities and the excitement of how they may be realized. The process leads to a positive attitude that actively seeks the desired outcome

- **Promoting learning.** Scenarios help people to understand their environment, consider the future, share knowledge, and evaluate strategic options. Information is better evaluated and integrated in the scenario planning process, which enables those involved in it to recognize and react to emerging circumstances

- **Creating a shared view.** Scenario thinking works because it looks beyond current assignments, facts, and forecasts. It allows discussions to be more uninhibited and it creates the conditions for a genuinely effective shared sense of purpose to evolve. Getting support for strategic decisions requires involving those that matter in the scenario planning process

ACTION CHECKLIST: SCENARIO PLANNING

The scenario thinking process is not one of linear implementation; its effectiveness lies in stimulating decisions, in the *strategic conversation*—a process that is refined with further environmental analysis.

> There are two things we can say for certain about the future. It will be different—and it will surprise.

1. **Planning and structuring the scenario process.** The first stage is to identify gaps in organizational knowledge that relate specifically to business challenges whose impact on the organization is uncertain. To do this, create a team to plan and structure the process. The team should probably come from outside the organization and its members should be noted for their creative thinking and ability to challenge conventional ideas. An external team is better placed to provide objective support, free from internal agendas or tensions. In discussion with the team, decide on the duration of the project; ten weeks is considered appropriate for a big project.

2. **Exploring the scenario context.** Team members should be interviewed to highlight the main views and to assess if these ideas are shared among different team members. Questions should focus on vital issues such as sources of customer value, the current success formula, and future challenges, identifying how each individual views the past, present, and future aspects of each issue. The interview statements should be collated and analyzed in an interview report, structured around the recurring concepts and key themes. This now sets the agenda for the first workshop and should be sent to all participants. It is also valuable to identify the critical uncertainties and issues, as perceived by the participants, as a starting point for the workshop.

3. **Developing the scenarios.** The workshop should identify the forces that will have an impact over an agreed period. Two possible opposite outcomes should be agreed and the forces that could lead to each of them should be listed. This will help to show how these forces link together. Next, decide whether each of these forces has a low or high impact and a low or high probability. This information should be displayed on a 2×2 matrix.

By clearly presenting two polar outcomes and all the driving forces, the team can then develop the likely "histories"—or scenarios—that led to each outcome. These histories of the future can then be expanded through discussion of the forces behind the changes. The aim is not to develop accurate predictions, but to understand what will shape the future and how different events interact and influence each other. All the time, discussions are focused on each scenario's impact on the organization.

This part of the process opens up the thinking of the members in the team and it makes them alert to signals that may suggest a particular direction for the organization. The outcomes of different responses are "tested" in the safety of scenario planning, avoiding the risk of implementing a strategy for real.

4. **Analyzing the scenarios.** The analysis stage examines the external issues and internal logic. Consider:

- What are the priorities and concerns of those outside the organization who are also responsible for the main decisions in the scenario?

- Who are the other stakeholders?

- Who are the key players and do they change?

- Would they really act and make decisions in the way described?

Systems and process diagrams can help address these questions, as can discussions with other stakeholders. Remember, we are not trying to pinpoint future events, but to consider the forces that may push the future along different paths.

5. **Using the scenarios.** Working backwards from the future to the present, the team should formulate an action plan that can influence the organization's thinking. Next, it should identify the early signs of change so that when they do occur, they will be recognized and responded to quickly and effectively. The process then continues by identifying gaps in organizational knowledge. The participatory and creative process sensitizes managers to the outside world. It helps individuals and teams to recognize the uncertainties in their operating environments so that they can question their everyday assumptions, adjust their mental maps, and think "outside the box."

CHECKLIST: ASSESSING BEHAVIORAL PROBLEMS AND CHALLENGES

Decision-making flaws are common in every organization. To assess the situation and start improving decision-making capabilities, it is helpful to consider the extent to which the hidden traps of decision making hamper the organization, by asking whether people regularly:

- Give disproportionate weight to the first piece of information they receive

- Seek to maintain the status quo

- Pursue failing decisions, in a forlorn attempt to recover past investments and credibility

- Seek confirming evidence to justify past or present decisions

- Display overconfidence

- Display excessive caution

- Incorrectly frame or state an issue—often leading to a flawed decision

- Give undue weight to a recent or dramatic event

- Procrastinate—delaying important decisions

As well as these common problems and behaviors, strategic decision making in groups is often hampered by groupthink and fragmentation.

- To what extent do these approaches affect key decisions?

- How prepared is your organization to drive and respond to change? Can you recall examples when the company has driven change, responded to it, or failed to do either? What are the reasons for this failure?

- What is the solution? (Understanding the root causes and then confronting them is the best approach—although this simple advice may often mask a complex and sensitive, even explosive, situation.)

PLANNING TO IMPROVE DECISION MAKING AND PROBLEM SOLVING

If you develop a personal action plan to improve decision making and problem solving, this should take account of the following challenges:

BALANCE ANALYSIS WITH THE NEED FOR ACTION

- Highlight major points in the data—keep to single words or one-liners

- Identify the critical detail required to make decisions

- Look for relationships and trends in the data

- Keep informed about relevant issues and trends with weekly updates, reports, and discussions with colleagues

- Build informal networks with colleagues and others outside the organization whose insight will be valuable later

- Establish a relationship with a mentor who can (a) help to develop decision-making skills, and (b) provide a sounding board when urgent decisions are needed

- Generate mutual understanding and respect with colleagues— especially those people whose information, position, and skills will be needed when you have a crucial decision to make

- Find out about incisive thinking techniques, such as Kepner-Tregoe analysis, lateral thinking, and mind mapping

BE PROACTIVE

Here are ten things that proactive decision makers and problem solvers do:

1. Question the appropriateness of previous decisions.

2. Involve stakeholders in making decisions to build commitment.

3. Actively search out information from a variety of sources.

4. Identify the non-negotiable constraints in a decision.

5. Search for a broad range of alternatives.

6. Look for long-term solutions.

7. Create new options by combining features of other options.

8. Figure out how to improve the best option and make it even better.

9. Ask "What could go wrong?" and plan preventive actions.

10. Anticipate and plan for future decision points.

Think about the decisions you make:

- Which of these ten things do you do consistently?

- Which of these ten things can you start doing more often?

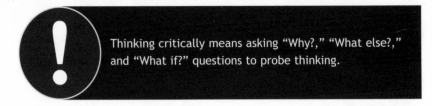

Thinking critically means asking "Why?," "What else?," and "What if?" questions to probe thinking.

It is also useful to:

- Challenge the thinking of others, even when they appear to be on firm ground

- Identify and challenge the assumptions or rationale that underpin decisions

- Get others to pinpoint the exact reasons for their views

- Challenge and provoke—look for radical change

- Play devil's advocate and go for the opposite of current practice

- Avoid acceptance of the status quo

IDENTIFY OPTIONS

This can be accomplished by brainstorming the available options and highlighting the most favorable ones. Techniques that can help include:

- Reducing your list of available options by ruling out those that miss some agreed criteria

- Identifying one vital question that if answered would provide the information needed to proceed—how can you get this answered?

- Calculating which option gives most benefit after taking into account the costs

- Using others' experiences to see how they would tackle the task

- Avoiding always choosing the easiest option

USE LATERAL THINKING

Find other ways of generating solutions and ideas by:

- Brainstorming ideas without criticizing them

- Saying something silly or provocative to get the creative juices flowing

- Drawing a picture to describe how things could change

- Avoiding a conservative or "safe" approach

CONCEPTUALIZE

Create an ideal picture of how you would like an issue to be resolved or progressed.

- Think of *what* you are trying to achieve not how you will achieve it

- Establish the end point in your mind—what the initiative will achieve—and work backward to see which method best achieves this goal

CONSIDER CUSTOMER NEEDS

The single biggest influence on entrepreneurial decisions is how it affects customers. Focusing on customers is a vital part of making the best decisions and it can be achieved by:

- Putting yourself in the customers' shoes and seeing areas of vital importance

- Brainstorming what you could do to best meet their needs and objectives

- Researching your intended changes to ensure that customers want them

- Prioritizing the list of actions that you need to take

- Avoiding assuming you know what the customer wants

- Finding out about the customers' aims and aspirations

- Looking to offer options to the customer in most standard situations

- Avoiding accepting without question the customers' first statement of need

- Looking for opportunities to talk informally to customers

- Following up on sales to see what happened post-sale

- Using customer feedback as evidence in making internal recommendations

- Anticipating customer needs, where appropriate, by taking time to review their long-term plans

MASTER THE ESSENTIALS

- Anticipate the impact of major decisions

- Find out about decision analysis techniques

- Keep informed about relevant issues and trends

- Build informal networks

- Deal with ambiguity and risk

- Take unpopular decisions when needed. This may mean you need to:
  - Prepare an honest explanation and keep putting the message over
  - Explain the implications of not taking the decision
  - Involve those affected by the decision wherever possible
  - Keep people informed of progress
  - Paint clear pictures of the desired result
  - Avoid delay or signs of personal uncertainty
  - Achieve consensus

FINALLY, ACCEPT PERSONAL RESPONSIBILITY

This may mean that you need to:

- Ask for comments from colleagues on the effectiveness of a recent decision or the way it was made

- Discuss and explicitly agree with your manager the extent of your decision-making responsibilities

- Talk through the expected outcome of a decision with your manager or team before making the decision—and remain accountable for the results

- Find a challenging issue and take responsibility for delivering an effective solution (working with others as necessary)

DOS AND DON'TS

DO:

- Clarify the issues, working out what is essential and what is desirable

- Consult widely to gain a comprehensive perspective

- Gather information and remain objective

- Look for other situations when similar solutions and ideas were required

- Review past situations—what worked, what failed, and why?

- Understand where the risks lie and take action to control and reduce these

- Communicate—people need to know what decisions are being made and why, if they are to be successful

- Challenge existing thinking and orthodoxy—brilliant decisions and solutions are rarely routine

DO NOT:

- Let personal preferences or preconceptions cloud your judgment

- Forget to consider implementation: decisions need to be pragmatic and workable

- Neglect to monitor or follow up decisions—decisions need constant attention and leadership. Don't just decide and never look back!

- Forget customers—what will the decision mean for them?

- Rush to an obvious decision or solution—a better alternative may exist

OTHER TITLES IN THE CAREER MAKERS SERIES

Detox Your Career
10 steps to revitalizing your job and career

Patrick Forsyth

ISBN 981 261 815 5 (Asia & ANZ)

ISBN 1-904879-51-9

UK £12.99 • USA $23.95 • CAN $32.95

OTHER TITLES IN THE CAREER MAKERS SERIES

Manage Your Boss
8 steps to creating the ideal working relationship

Patrick Forsyth

ISBN 981 261 820 1 (Asia & ANZ)

ISBN 1-904879-53-5

UK £12.99 • USA $23.95 • CAN $32.95

OTHER TITLES IN THE CAREER MAKERS SERIES

New Kid on the Block
10 steps to help you survive and thrive
in the first 100 days of your new job

Frances Kay

ISBN 981 261 821 X (Asia & ANZ)

ISBN 1-904879-52-7

UK £12.99 • USA $23.95 • CAN $32.95